"This is more than an academic read; it is a real how-to book that will benefit those in and out of the academic sphere. The writing touched me in so many ways as it brought to bear issues I have faced as a student, a black male, and a CEO. What I most appreciated was the way that the author exposed her true self as a means of helping the reader understand her viewpoint. This book is truly a must read for those who call themselves or seek to become leaders."

— *Damyn Kelly, PhD, JD, President and CEO, Lutheran Social Services of New York, USA*

"As former dean of a social work school, I spent a lot of time working with students, faculty, and staff on three central ideas that are also a core part of this important book: How do we get students and faculty to understand the importance of thinking comprehensively about race and racism? Are there ways to short-circuit hard and fast distinctions between theory and practice, and between macro and clinical scales of analysis/intervention, so that people recognize and mobilize the inextricable links between them? And are there ways to reframe discussions of diversity and inclusion that truly address the foundational traumas caused by America's most fundamental commitments to racial hierarchies and exclusions? *Incorporating Diversity and Inclusion into Trauma-Informed Social Work* does a masterful job of tackling all three of these questions—and more—by showing their interrelated nature and pushing us beyond our commonsensical assumptions about how we talk, work, counsel, create policy, and lead institutions in the context of the many forms of difference that define our social world. This is a very powerful book, and I can't wait to use it in my own work as a scholar and an administrator."

—*John L. Jackson, Jr., PhD, Richard Perry University Professor, University of Pennsylvania, USA*

"This is a timely and highly relevant book for anyone interested in the fields of trauma or leadership. Dr. Laura Quiros uses her personal narrative, research, and professional experiences to fill a void in the trauma field by addressing structural racism in the trauma narrative. Dr. Quiros uses her own story to explore trauma informed practice through a lens of diversity and equity. Embedded in the work is a discussion of the COVID-19 pandemic as an example of the need for transformational leadership to address racial trauma. Her story as a trauma survivor, combined with her experiences of racism and anti-Semitism and her professional work as a clinician and academic, make this an important read for understanding the connections of trauma, inclusion, and social justice."

Lisa M. Najavits, PhD, Director,
Treatment Innovations, Adjunct Professor,
University of Massachusetts Medical School, USA

INCORPORATING DIVERSITY AND INCLUSION INTO TRAUMA-INFORMED SOCIAL WORK

Incorporating Diversity and Inclusion into Trauma-Informed Social Work incorporates discussions of leadership, racism and oppression into a new understanding of how trauma and traumatic experience play out in leadership and organizational cultures.

Chapters unpack ideas about the intersections of self, trauma and leadership, bridging the personal and professional, and illustrating the relationship between employees and leaders. Discussion questions and reflections at the end of each chapter offer the opportunity for the reader to understand their own vulnerabilities in relation to the subject matter. This book reconceptualizes cultural competency, trauma and leadership in the context of the 2020 COVID-19 pandemic and views theories and practices through a lens of diversity and inclusivity.

Incorporating Diversity and Inclusion into Trauma-Informed Social Work is an expansive guide for students in social work, one that explores and explains how trauma and difference manifest in how we communicate, lead and work with each other.

Laura Quiros, PhD, LMSW, is an associate professor of social work at Adelphi University and a trauma-informed diversity, equity and inclusion consultant. She teaches social work at the doctoral and master's levels.

INCORPORATING DIVERSITY AND INCLUSION INTO TRAUMA-INFORMED SOCIAL WORK

Transformational Leadership

Laura Quiros

Routledge
Taylor & Francis Group
NEW YORK AND LONDON

First published 2021
by Routledge
52 Vanderbilt Avenue, New York, NY 10017

and by Routledge
2 Park Square, Milton Park, Abingdon, Oxon, OX14 4RN

Routledge is an imprint of the Taylor & Francis Group, an informa business

Library of Congress Cataloging-in-Publication Data
A catalog record for this title has been requested

ISBN: 978-0-367-24725-6 (hbk)
ISBN: 978-0-367-24724-9 (pbk)
ISBN: 978-0-429-28440-3 (ebk)

Typeset in Sabon
by KnowledgeWorks Global Ltd.

CONTENTS

PREFACE

This research, at its core, is a project in intentional, positive disruption of trauma-informed practice, and diversity and inclusion. I share my experiences and research with the social work community and leaders in the field of human services in an effort to teach, train and live in a world where positive disruption, complexity and vulnerability become valued and normative. Here, in this goal-oriented process and work, lies the intentionality. I desire a way of being for the social work and leadership community that is grounded in trauma-informed practice. However, my personal definition and application of trauma-informed practice deviates from the established norm as it includes and emphasizes socio-political traumas. In this project I introduce and work through a practice that I call "intentional positive disruption" that I use to disrupt common foundational terms of social work and status quos. It is via this practice of positive disruption that I disrupt the traditional practice and understanding of trauma to include socio-political traumas. The way of being I have taught in Universities and in consulting requires students to engage in this work from a place of humility, vulnerability, compassion, sincerity and higher order purpose. Operating from this way of being makes room for sincere inclusion and diversity, fostering an intentional connection to the social justice mission that social work is grounded in.

We generally see and respond to the world through our individual lens that is grounded in our personal histories and familial ways of knowing. We are the sum total of our experiences and for some of us, familial experiences and values impact career choice. In fact, I find that especially with social work, students often choose the profession of social work because of a family trauma or event, including the traumas of marginalization and oppression. I certainly know I did, and it is my practice in life and in this project to locate myself before starting class, dialogues, workshops or trainings. Locating myself involves a process of discussing and bringing into the world personal experiences and narratives which I feel are of relevance to the topic at hand, and carry influence over how I may see or interpret said topic. In regards to social work, students enter the field and "give back," to heal, seek repair, or make up for past traumas often that remain outside of personal control. These range from interpersonal traumas to socio-political traumas. Although we, as social workers, may be conscious of this choice in profession, we are not always conscious of the narratives created from past experiences that drive behaviors, drive our social work practice and leadership styles, and impact growth. Even more, once realized, then what? Do we stop there or do we engage in continual self-reflection as we encounter new and repeated traumas, new clients, receive promotions, enter into supervisory and other leadership positions? Do we use that self-knowledge to reflect on and engage with the ways we are upholding the core values of social work, specifically social justice? Do we also engage in a process of self-reflection that includes how we have been upholding the values of the status quo and the dominating white discourse, despite our social justice mandate? The field of social work gives us, as social workers, the opportunity to positively disrupt exclusive spaces that further marginalize our clients and communities, grow personally and professionally, heal, build relationships with individuals, groups and communities and share ourselves in ways unlike any other profession.

Locating Myself

I typically begin my trauma narrative at the age of six. I had a brother who passed away on Christmas Eve from Sudden Infant Death

Syndrome (SIDS). My aunt was home watching over my brother and I, and I remember her saying she had to take care of something and would be right back. I was home alone for enough time to check on him, notice that he was not breathing and as a result, had turned blue in his crib. I imagine we all have had those moments when we feel in our bodies that something is wrong, that unarticulated, intuitive and visceral knowledge. My mom returned home shortly after my discovery to confirm my finding that he had stopped breathing. The image of her running down the stairs holding Daniel in her arms while screaming "*my baby isn't breathing*" has faded but I can draw upon it at any moment. My aunt came back in time for us to pile into the white jeep in the snow and ice and rush to the hospital. As a six-year-old child who felt in control and independent enough to be home alone with her baby brother, to then witness his death just hours later, was devastating. For many years, I lived under the spell of magical thinking, what if I checked on him earlier? What could I have done to prevent his death? I developed the symptoms that are most common after a traumatic event; hyper-vigilance, fear that something bad would happen every time I was alone, anxiety and flashbacks. I have a vivid memory of sitting with Daniel on a wooden rocking chair weeks before he passed and saying to him "*I love you and hope nothing bad ever happens*." And then it did. As a child my coping mechanism was to play make-believe to keep Daniel alive in my mind and then as I got older, he was the subject of every creative writing assignment. As for my post-trauma reactions to Daniel's passing, I left my post-trauma responses alone for enough time for them to manifest in other areas of my life. Some manifestations were positive, such as sports and school and others were not. I went to college on a sports scholarship and decided to major in psychology. Following college, I worked as a mental health consultant at a psychiatric hospital for children in upstate New York for a few years before making the decision to return to school for social work. What drove my decision was the social work person in environment framework coupled with social justice mission of the profession. Many of the kids in the hospital were kids of color who had grown up in the inner city and for many reasons found themselves in a psychiatric hospital in update New York. I wanted to help "save" kids in their environments. I ultimately pursued a Masters in

Social Work (MSW) at Hunter College School of Social Work. Clear in all of these decisions is that my purpose for years was to save children and find a better ending to my story, one where I was the savior.

Positive Disruption

This leads us to my first encounter with positive disruption. This occurred when my social policy professor in my MSW program told me I was never going to save children, and that as long as I made this field about me, I would never develop my sense of self and reach any higher order purpose, but instead stay stuck in my story. On that very first day of class, with this statement in front of my peers, he disrupted my childhood narrative and my path. His sincere response to my confession of why I wanted to pursue an MSW was jarring, uncomfortable and transformational. It may sound odd that this moment was met with so much acceptance from me. I think for some, the direct and confrontational response may have caused a defense rebuttal, perhaps a pushing back or even a withdrawal and disengagement, but for me it was the opposite. I was hungry for guidance and looked to higher education to guide me, so in retrospect, I was open to exploring what this professor offered me in this moment of disruption. He was also a highly respected and well-known white male. Furthermore, I was especially open and accepting of this disruption because at that time in my development my racial identity was undefined, I was struggling with issues of validation and acceptance at home with my own father, and I had bought into the higher education reverence of the white male figure. Because the classroom is not a neutral place, I believe his positionality was significant to my openness. For those of you sitting in classrooms right now, how do you experience your instructors? How does positionality play out in the classroom? I think this is especially important to reflect on for white students being taught by professors of color. How are you seeing them and hearing them?

That initial encounter with what I define as positive disruption lifted me out of my narrative that was unconsciously driving so much of my behavior. Daniel's death was the catalyst of my lifetime journey. It was a traumatic childhood experience that ultimately delivered me to the world of social work. However, once I was mentally, emotionally and intellectually able to work through my professors' disruption in the classroom, I was able to understand that it would be my love of connection, my desire to honor complexity in the human condition, my drive for social justice and inclusion, and my healing that would keep me and allow me to thrive in the social work profession. "Working through" this disruption meant first listening to what he said, taking it in, noticing the "sting" and the immediate reaction to shrink and move away from his words and then reflect on my journey up until the moment I decided to pursue an MSW. Working through this disruption required the help of therapy and education. The combination of personal work, literature, research, my internships and new relationships with my classmates and professors, all at once, moved me along my journey.

My work looks to nuance traditional definitions and understandings of this concept and action of disruption because I find it often carries a negative connotation. Meaning, traditional definitions and understandings of disruption evoke fear of entering a space of liminality that feels uncomfortable and unsettling, and is a rupture to the system characterized by uncertainty, ambiguity and disturbance. Instead, I see disruption as an action that involves making room for more, more nuance, more complexity, more inclusion. In this project, positive disruption is just that, making room for more. That is, positive disruption is an inclusive practice that involves mindfulness, courage, curiosity, compassion and vulnerability, the impact of which is personal evolution and ultimately leadership transformation.

The outcomes I have found in my teaching, scholarship and consulting is that positively disrupting traditional definitions of trauma to be more encompassing; positively disrupting traditional notions of leadership to be vulnerable and welcome vulnerability; and positively disrupting the boundary between what is traditionally conceived as personal experience and professional experience has led to the creation of a work space that is healthier, and therefore more productive. Because my work positively disrupts these boundaries and teaches how to positively disrupt boundaries, I have found better and longer lasting results and relationships. Rather than teaching to scenarios which may be unrealistic or awkward, I am teaching and helping to develop a mindset and a way of being that is truly *inclusive*.

ACKNOWLEDGEMENTS

Writing this book was an incredibly vulnerable and healing process. So much different than the peer review article process. It was exposing and raw and served as both a reminder of traumas I have not talked about for years, and healing that I still had to do. I could not have done any of this without my brother Julian. In the course of writing this book Julian became my research assistant, my editor and my guide. He helped me garner the courage to push through when I most needed it. He assisted me with creating and crafting my narrative for you, the reader, to learn from. He pushed me to move beyond the self-doubt and anger that I was still harboring in areas of my life, to a place of ownership of my word and compassion. I want to thank him and wish him strength as he enters his PhD program in the fall of 2020. I hope he can also share this project with his professors and colleagues as something that he was central in crafting.

My daughters, Isabel and Carla are my heart space. The two people who always force me to do better as a woman and as a mother. Isabel's spirit helps me center revolutionary love and Carla's grace and wisdom helps guide me. I would like to acknowledge all of the work my mother has done on her own whiteness. She served as a reader in this process, always honoring my work and my need to name many of the traumas we experienced as a family. My partner, Lloyd Crawford created the stability in our home that was necessary for me to write and complete this project. I deeply value his love, kindness and ease that was a stabilizing force in this journey. My social justice educators who came before me, my community of women friends, my colleagues who are also near and dear to my heart and help guide me in particular: Dr. CarolAnn Daniel, Dr. Beverly Araujo-Dawson, Dr. Rani Varghese and Dr. Todd Vanidestine, thank you. A special thanks to the organizations and leaders who trusted me with their staff and with themselves. Our work is deeply personal to me. Some of you have become lifelong friends that I am so grateful for because it is these relationships that keep me going. I would also like to thank my mentors and educators throughout my life, in particular, Dr. Michael Fabricant, Dr. Joe Kincheloe, Dr. Andrea Savage, Dr. Sharon Cadiz, Dr. Harriet Goodman, Dr. Mimi Abramovitz, Dr. Lisa Najavits, Dr. Sharon Cadiz, Dean John Jackson Jr., Dr. Michael Funk, Dr. Perry Greene and Dr. Mary Pender Greene. I would also like to acknowledge the leaders of Montclair YMCA and specifically, Kimberly Marsh and Mike Chiles my Montclair community YMCA Diversity, Equity and Inclusion co-chairs; and all of the students I have shared space with. I would also like to thank the people who made specific contributions in this book, namely Dr. Todd Vanidestine, Dr. Damyn Kelly, Natalie Brooks-Wilson, Shavone Hamilton, Kat Myers and Genie Colbert. Finally, my father's spirit lives in this project, in every chapter and on every page.

Contributors

Julian Quiros: (helped with editing and process)
Dr. Damyn Kelly (endorser): (shared experiences within document) CEO, Lutheran Social Services of New York
Dr. Todd Vanidestine: Assistant Professor, West Chester University (shared classroom experience in document Chapter 1)
Kat Myers: (case study) head of HR Respondent

Genie Colbert: (case study) head of HR Sanctuary for Families
Natalie Brooks Wilson: (case study) PhD. candidate, Adelphi University
Shavone Hamilton: (research assistant) PhD. candidate, Adelphi University

INTRODUCTION

Locating Myself in Purpose

My impetus for this project is both personal and professional. Using my lens as a researcher, practitioner, trauma survivor, mother and woman of color from a multiracial and multiethnic background, I identified a deficiency and an interconnectedness in fields of trauma, diversity and inclusion, and social work leadership. I share with you my multitudinal identity because I do not and cannot have a separate or distinct lens un-influenced by the world. My ultimate aim for this book is to teach you, the reader, how to use yourself to be a more intentional, mindful and positively disruptive social work student and a transformational leader in a diversity of spaces. I will do that by positively disrupting personal and professionals' realms. This book is geared toward students in the social work profession but my hope is that this book, and its work, is relevant to all who are seeking to introduce increased understanding, mindfulness, compassion and vulnerability into the way they not just understand diversity and inclusion but live it…I begin with my personal journey that lead me to this project.

Locating Myself: My Story as a Model for Practice

Personally, I identify as a Latina and Jewish woman of color. My pronouns are she/her/hers. My mother is a white and Jewish woman, and my father Black and Latino. My mother and I do not share the same racial identity and I have watched her over the years operate in ways that are very much connected to her privilege as a white woman. Some specific examples I recall include; her friends were always white women, she moved with ease in grocery stores sometimes even unconsciously steeping in front of people, she had no problem asking several times when our table or food would be ready in restaurants, and I remember seeing her talk her way out of more than one traffic ticket. These unearned advantages are similar to the privileges Peggy McIntosh writes about in her article White Privilege; Unpacking the Invisible White Knapsack (McIntosh, 1988). I distinctly remember reading this article in graduate school and thinking of my mother. Growing up I was physically uncomfortable in the moments she operated from a place of privilege, but I struggled with why. We never spoke about the unearned advantages she received because of the color of her skin until somewhat recently in my late thirties. Having a conversation with my mother about our distinct lived experiences was an uncharted territory for me. The felt precariousness associated with this decision, to claim an identity as one different from hers, and hold her accountable for the ways she unconsciously navigated the world through a lens of white privilege was real for me. Her unconscious navigation of her privilege weighed heavy on our relationship, and sometimes it still does. I am not granted the same white privileges as my mom and so there was, and still is, a stress producing uneasiness when she operated and operates in entitled ways. The dissonance in the ways racial identity lived and lives in us and between us affected and affects our relationship. Even with my felt tension between us, I was still unsure how to approach this divide with her. It was as if I was walking the line of self-proclamation and abandonment, or invalidation in the most immediate. Holding my mother accountable and claiming my identity as a woman of color to my white mother felt like a political act for me, one that I was not able to take on until after I received my Masters in Social Work. Equipped with the language, education, degree, a new community of friends who also occupied biracial and bicultural spaces, mentors who challenged me and my personal therapy, I had the permission and the tools to begin the process of naming and claiming my whole self. I gave her Robin DiAngelo's book *White Fragility* (DiAngelo, 2018) to read and I began to slowly hold her accountable during those moments when I witnessed her using her white privilege. To this day, it is not always easy to call these behaviors out in empathic ways and sometimes I choose to stay silent. There remains dissonance between us as our lived experiences as women, who are racially and culturally different will always be a thing for me. I think this dissonance speaks to our distinct racial identities and racial and cultural traumas that live in our bodies not necessarily our minds. For so many years so much was left unsaid and so many experiences of unearned white privilege and racial and cultural oppression were denied. I am reminded of Resmaa Menakem's book *My Grandmothers' Hands* (Menakem, 2017) and his testaments to the lived and felt experience of fear, hope and trauma. I am also reminded of the opportunity as a parent to promote, facilitate and nurture conversations about racial and cultural identity early in my daughters' lives.

Learning to live in between the binaries of Black and white was an early lesson in understanding the complexity of people in relationships and in understanding the enactment of race and culture. While feeling disconnected to my mother in one sense, I was also able to hold on tight to her valuable lesson of relationship building. It was my mother who taught me about learning the world through relationships. She always had a circle of tight knit women friends and I watched her lean into them during the most difficult times of her marriage. My parents divorced during my adolescence. It was an ugly divorce, the kind that was fraught with alcoholism, infidelity, domestic violence and mental illness, all manifestations of undealt with personal and relational trauma. It was the recognition of the personal and familial trauma I was surrounded by growing up that led me to approach my inclusivity work with a trauma-informed lens. Specifically, the coupling of the trauma between my parents, with the trauma of naming myself in spaces where my identities were divorced and the psychological freedoms of that act were not there, created the conditions that lead me to approach my work in this way. Marrying and curating different aspects of different approaches, practices and lenses led me to practice and teach social work in the way that I do. Part of this project is healing, recognizing and coming to terms with unhealthy relationships with people, society and interpersonal life. This is not possible without allowing others to also provide justification for conscious or unconscious behavior.

People in my life have referenced my ability to work with, teach and get along with so many different types of people. I had to. I survived by negotiating many different worlds, worlds that did not and do not accept or understand one another. Often times, at a young age, I occupied a space where one aspect of my identity was inside while the other was outside. It was almost as if my body was split into factions and so much of the inclusion and exclusion was based on my physicality, which was totally void of my complexities and nuance as a bicultural and biracial woman. Living on the Borderlands, as Gloria Anzaldua (Anzaldua, 1987) discusses, helped me understand the complexity, nuance and multi-faceted ways in which inclusion could simultaneously be exclusionary, and the racialization that accompanies it.

While to this day, spaces in my personal and professional worlds continue to attempt to fracture my identity and complexity, through my lived experience I have learned how to introduce compassion, nuance and understanding into these spaces; increasing my comfort in the moment, while hopefully mitigating attempts at fracturing on the part of the other participants in the future. Introducing nuance, compassion and awareness into these spaces requires a use self and an intentional mindset of creating opportunities for commonalities among people while also recognizing, naming and validating the pain of exclusion among Black, Indigenous and people of color (BIPOC) and the shame of denial and exclusion among white people. To be more specific, traditionally in my line of work and the work of the social work field, white people are often in denial of racial traumas in the lived experience of Black, Indigenous and people of color. White people don't see it because they don't have to. The denial might lead to internal feelings of embarrassment, shame, guilt and definitely the exclusion of difference. But to be clear, dependent on the context and actors, anyone who is wielding the more powerful position is capable of being an excluder. "If ultimately, humanity exists only through being in and of the world, can we find a relation with others based on the reciprocal recognition of our common vulnerability and finitude?" (Mbembe, 2019) In this project, I attempt to do just that, find a place of common vulnerability and finitude. I think we can all reflect and share examples of how our inclusion or presence in one space has allowed the people we are with to conflate, ignore and openly exclude people who share other facts of our identity.

My grandfather, my mom's dad, Papa, as we called him, did not believe in interracial marriage, despite my parents' union. Up until months before he passed away, we engaged in more than one conversation about his conviction that "white people should not marry Black people." He did not support my parents' marriage and worked hard to keep them apart in the beginning of their courtship. His racism and anti-Black sentiment played out in many ways in my relationship with him and also in the community where he lived. As a child, it was confusing to be loved but not accepted. He was so kind and loving to me, while simultaneously also being and acting explicitly racist in many facets of his life. When visiting my Nana and Papa's home in Boca Raton Florida, I was told by their neighbors, who were also their friends, on more than once occasion, to get out of the pool because I was "too dark" to swim in their pool. The few times I did attend a synagogue, I remember feeling very uncomfortable in the sea of whiteness and privilege of that whiteness that surrounded me. And on the other side, the anti-Semitism from my father and my fathers' side was real, mostly in the form of jokes and intense stereotyping. Those slips of the tongue in the form of jokes that inflict violence, injure, humiliate and remind me that I am not one of them (Mbembe, 2019). The jokes about Jews hurt more because being Jewish was conflated with being white and from my father, it felt like a rejection of my identity as Latina and as a woman of color. At that time, I did not have knowledge of the history of Black Judaism and although I participated in the strict traditions and observances shared by my mothers' family, I always felt on the outside, surrounded by whiteness and racism. There was no space for me to share these feelings or ask uncomfortable questions, as a young child still negotiating feelings of identity, I was not yet aware that this is space I would need to create. My parents were not comfortable with their own racial and cultural identities and so this left me on my own with some very complicated feelings. My healing process for many years involved a back and forth of rejection and acceptance of my multiple identities and my parents. I continue to heal my traumas of exclusivity by learning to build relationships with a diverse array of people, expand the socially constructed markers of identity and create truly inclusive spaces. I use myself and the narratives of my identity and daily experiences as a model for social work practice, and teach my social work students to do the same. The sharing of self is not normative in social work practice. In fact, students are often told not to "disclose" and sometimes encouraged to stay emotionally disconnected from the client. Yet, the lived experiences of the practitioner and the client live in the room, in the session and in the group. Instead of a strict adherence to boundaries, social work practice would benefit from an intentional focus on intentional sharing and centering the power of vulnerability that leads to a deeper connection. I have been told in my work that I sincerely and generously share myself with my audience, with the intention of freeing them up to do the same.

I am also a single mother of two young girls, who at the time of writing this are ages 6 and 12 years old. I share this part of myself because the disruption around identity, as it relates to my identity as a single mother, has been and continues to be a journey. On bar to my multicultural and biracial background, my identity as a single mother who has been divorced twice, has a stereotype and social construction attached to it that is both negative and hard to wiggle out of. The intersectionality of my cultural and racial identity, and single motherhood brings with it a host of assumptions centered on me and on my girls. What I find most healing is watching and listening to my 12-year-old explain to her friends without any hesitation that her and her sister have 2 different dads. Her comfort in living outside of the boundaries of tradition is incredible. While I embrace the paradox of my personal life, I am always negotiating how much of myself to bring into a space. I find myself wanting to bring in my whole self, while thinking that judgment waits on the other end. For example, sharing this narrative of disrupting the institution of marriage is complicated for others to hear and make sense of. Most of the time, this narrative becomes about the other person instead of engaging in a sincere act of sharing in an attempt to learn about me, and what prevails are assumptions and judgements. I do not have it all figured out and I embrace the ambiguous and uncomfortable spaces where I still need to heal, grow while trying to integrate the learnings into my teaching. I am taking more risks in sharing this part of me in an effort to live by teachings and practice of vulnerability.

Locating Myself Professionally

Professionally, I am in my 11th year in academia having served as an Assistant Professor, Associate Dean of Academic Affairs and currently as an Associate Professor. In addition, I consult for both for- and non-profit organizations, helping executive leaders and leadership teams create more inclusive and diverse organizational cultures through a trauma-informed lens.

In the past few years, I have been given a wealth of opportunities to work with a diversity of organizations; The Documentary Group, Respondent, Billie, brooklinen, Konica Minolta, The New School, Immunomedics, Administration for Children Services, PricewaterhouseCoopers, Sanctuary for Children, Partnership with Children, Staten Island Legal Services, Y7 Studio, New York Pilates and my own Adelphi University. Each one of these organizations has provided me with learning opportunities and relationships that have deepened my work. They range in size and sector; from large non-profits, to small for-profit start-ups, in addition to work in academic institutions. The intersectionality of my identities as well as my combined experience of being a trained social work clinician and an educator with a trauma-informed, diversity and inclusion lens, make me well positioned to enter a breadth of organizations. Something social workers should consider early in their careers is the diversity of opportunities that are available beyond the traditional social work field. So many organizations are hungry to engage in deeper work and learn how to foster more compassionate, inclusive and trauma-informed organizational cultures. When working with and for these companies I strive to bring my whole self to each space in the spirit of compassion and accountability. I am so appreciative that the leaders of these organizations let me into their worlds to build relationships with employees and supervisors at many levels of the organization and help them better connect to themselves and missions of diversity and inclusion. My life experiences and narrative, I believe, gives me an understanding of the struggles white executives have with becoming aware of the normalcy and ordinariness of whiteness in the workplace and our American culture. As an example, the conversation I had with my mom discussing the feelings that surfaced for me as a mother of color when she bought my Black daughter a white barbie doll has similar parallels to what I try to bring to light in these organizations and in their leaders. Negotiating the black and white binaries allows me to enter spaces with a compassion for and awareness of the diverse lived experiences of my clients. I realize that despite the differences in clientele and organizational structure, there remains a common thread of the need to belong, human connection and relationship building. There is also a common thread of fear of vulnerability, exposure and pressure to "get it right." My work with all of my clients involves a deep dive into the challenges associated with locating themselves in an effort to connect with the practices of diversity and inclusion through a trauma-informed lens, and how so much of the entrance into this space is impacted by previous lived experiences and socialization. The false dichotomy of personal and professional does not exist in the workplace, and our work seeks to dispel this myth. The work is both personal and professional because I ask that folks first locate and sit with themselves to better reflect on how they lead and how they gather. For many leaders, this is a new practice. After building a relationship, which is a process involving listening, self-compassion, courage and mutual vulnerability, I present them with new ways of knowing and facilitate a process of integration that involves an awareness of the self in order to deepen self-awareness to allow new ways of knowing and action into their worlds and into their leadership styles. Part of our work involves making time and creating spaces to dialogue around how to let go of ways that stop them from leading with their hearts and minds and making connections that include, but are not limited to, past narratives, social constructions of leadership and precarity.

These usually take the form of individual coaching sessions that last anywhere from 45 minutes to two hours and take place in person, over the phone or via Zoom. Our work involves mindfulness, trust, vulnerability, nurturing, compassion and positive disruption. As my relationships with these organizations grow, I will continue to find the intersectionality in all of these worlds and always feel grateful for these opportunities. What emerges in our relationship is an awareness, self-compassion, compassion for others, courage, a vulnerability of just being and ultimately a sense of freedom that comes with the practice of accountability.

The Focus of This Project

Situated in the zeitgeist of our times of COVID-19 and the resurgence of the Black Lives Matter movement, this project takes on the very necessary and overdue task of intersecting and disrupting traditional notions and concepts of social work, leadership and trauma. Social work, in particular, is uniquely situated to be a leader in this moment. A field of practice grounded in the mission of social justice, I would argue that the social work profession has a responsibility to be a leader in this space characterized by inequity, vast economic and social disparity, and racial and cultural trauma. Even immediately prior to COVID-19 and the resurgence of the Black Lives Matter movement these were times when institutions and organizations were seeking to adopt and own missions of diversity, equity and inclusion for economic, moral, aesthetic and liability reasons. In my work as a consultant I have seen organizations adopt mission statements with all the right "hallmarks" of "making the world a better place," (Bryant, 2018). As Howard Bryant so rightly explains in his book *The Heritage*, "activism in the post-Ferguson American became as trendy as Patriotism," (p. 214). Supporting this statement was a cover story in the New York Times Style Section on November 21, 2019 (Zelevansky, 2019) titled "The Business of Unconscious Bias Training." I never thought work centered on inclusivity would find its place on the front page of the New York Times Style section. In another example, a recent article in The Guardian (Wheeler,

2020), highlights the initiative by Barnes & Noble to change the covers of classic novels to honor Black History Month, calling it the new "Diverse Editions" series. Twelve classic young adult novels were to receive new "culturally diverse" covers. The move was another showcasing of the trend to superficially fix the larger, historic and structural problem of race in America.

In my time as a diversity, equity and inclusion consultant and as an Associate Dean and Associate Professor at a private university, I witness folks really trying to figure it out, as if creating inclusive spaces with diverse staff and students is a piece of a puzzle or a riddle that one has a solve. They yearn for and prefer a handbook or checklist, rather than take the time to sit quietly and dive deep into their histories and hold themselves accountable. There is not a checklist for becoming more inclusive. Stepping away from the organizational setting for a moment, we see a mental health crisis across college campuses. Addressing the mental health needs of students involves a closer look at how colleges and universities have also operated in spaces of denial of racial trauma and many of the systems in place are void of holistic approaches for diverse student bodies. Colleges and universities are struggling to address the mental health needs of first-year students in particular. It is easy to forget that first year and transfer students bring their identities and family histories with them to college. Michael Lindsey, a mental health researcher and executive director of the McSilver Institute for Poverty Policy and Research at New York University states, "the traditional college stresses — the pressure to succeed, being on your own for the first time — can trigger the trauma lingering just below the surface" (Lindsey, 2019). Entering unfamiliar spaces, the balance and juggling of classes, being thrust into courses that are strictly discipline focused and not in tune with the First Year self in context can all be traumatic. And for students of color in predominately white institutions, the ordinariness of whiteness and white organizational culture is pervasive. This is even more relevant to Social Work education as a large proportion of our students are persons of color, and in the professional world that is reflected as well. However, at the leadership level in academia and practice – that is not reflected.

Although the college setting is considered and thought about differently from the work place, the relationships between peers, and between actor and institution is very similar. Furthermore, even with these similarities, trauma, depression and stress are viewed and treated very differently, one where the institution attempts (successful or not) to some extent to provide supports and another where largely these are all seen as personal problems to be dealt with outside of the productive space. Even the profession of social work warns against "personal disclosure" and we see the social construction of what it means to be both professional and productive as a disconnection from the self.

Expecting, or operating under the assumption, that lifelong and current traumas can be left at the front door by employees is unrealistic and unconducive to a healthy, productive work environment. This stands especially for Black, Indigenous and employees of color. Being a Black, Indigenous and person of color in a predominately white space is traumatic in and of itself. The world is a racialized place and white supremacy is deeply rooted in the history of this country. To think that the racism and anti-Black sentiment does not seep into the organizational culture is a misnomer. Increasingly, leaders in a host of different organizations and institutions are recognizing that fact. Yet, unlike technical skills, inclusion and implicit bias cannot be taught, sustained or, in the case of implicit bias, unlearned through run of the mill trainings and with outdated workplace behavior videos.

Conversations and trainings focused on diversity and inclusion are now more commonplace, but money and ubiquity do not guarantee long lasting results that require structural change. Research suggests diversity trainings do not work (Gassam, 2019). We then must ask, is this because diversity trainings are not being conducted effectively, or because its goal is unattainable? Recent articles such as the one in Forbes magazine written by Gassam (2019) highlight that simply training on unconscious bias does not counter trauma and the traumatized. "What unconscious bias trainings don't account for are the systemic and structural issues that allow biases to be perpetuated in the workplace." What message is this sending? And what opportunity does this create?

Moving Beyond the Performative

I see this moment as an opportunity for intentional and positive disruption that moves diversity and inclusion work away from the performative while incorporating a trauma-informed approach. What I mean by performative is beyond the language found in mission statements and strategic plans, where diversity and inclusion are words emptily emphasized; beyond the rules and quotas that prompt the hiring of leaders of color merely for quantitative publicity; and beyond the status quo where white organizational culture remains. That is, diversity and inclusion become more than just an optical phenomenon (Kapuku, 2019). For example, I push back, from a place of curiosity, when I start working with an organization and there is an immediate drive to create a mission statement. My question to the organization is, how do we craft a mission statement around diversity and inclusion when we do not even know how we are defining these terms or what we are working with? Language may serve as a place holder, but language alone does not translate into action. With one organization in particular, we are only now forming a diversity and inclusion mission statement after almost 2 years of consistently working together because staff from various levels of the organization have created an organizational culture that embraces inclusivity on every level, while also holding one another empathically accountable. Because this work is fluid and brave, it has allowed for first the vision and then the creation of a mission statement in which employees not only feel a connection to, but also one that they can personally define and put into their own words. So much of the hard work was envisioning a new, staying engaged with one another and being brave enough to speak truth to that vision. All of these conditions allow for and are conducive to normalizing an inclusive organizational culture across time and through employee turnover.

Vulnerability

Throughout this book I model transparency and vulnerability, as I do when I teach, consult, parent and am in relationships. Vulnerability becomes normative when you consciously and intentionally continue to make yourself vulnerable to and in different situations. Because I am vulnerable as the author of this book, I am fallible and I challenge you, the reader, to disrupt claims I make as you read. The intentional, positive disruption I would like you to use with this project can be applied anywhere and therefore this theoretical framework of "disruption" is an interdisciplinary value.

I see this process as part of the learning and part of the product. With a few exceptions, tradition teaches us, as authors, researchers and professors to remain disconnected. Yet the true disconnection of author positionality and subject, is not only impossible, but also leaves a gap for students. Telling your story gives people permission to tell theirs. There is so much power in narratives because it brings another persons' world in the space of truth. Sharing narratives allows for others in the room to see and hear emotional and experienced based commonalities and create connection which otherwise may not have been possible. The field of social work is grounded in connection and relationship building. We ask clients and executives to share the most intimate struggles and be reflective of those struggles. As educators in positions of power, we must do the same. One goal for this book is to make vulnerability, transparency and accountability normative as a way to deepen human connection and belonging. Writing from a personal place is valuable because it connects students to the material in a deeper, more intimate way and gives permission for students to do the same, in the classroom, in supervision and in the field with their clients. It is my hope that such practices will ultimately lead to truly inclusive spaces that are trauma-informed and guided by social justice.

In the following chapters, I aim to present examples of positive disruption, a re-conceptualization of specific terms, a definition of transformational leadership and its accompanying traits, and discuss some challenges and tools to positively disrupt while validating the precarity[1] (Butler, 2015) that comes with speaking truth to power. Regarding this last point, often in white heteronormative patriarchal spaces, marginalized communities are the ones to be pegged to describe what discrimination and marginalization feels like, and then tasked with how to fix it. This often occurs without an analysis or discussion of the normalization of whiteness in body and ideology. In Butler's words, "Precarity is the rubric that brings together women, queers, transgender people, the poor, the differently abled and the stateless, but also religious and racial minorities; it is a social and economic condition, but not an identity. Indeed, it cuts across these categories and produces potential alliances among those who do not recognize that they belong to one another" (Butler, 2015, p. 58). In support of Butlers' work, I use the concept of precarity as a unifying condition among marginalized populations whose lives are not protected and remain at risk of economic insecurity and physical and psychological violence because of the dominant social structures and neoliberal values of society. Not all bodies are equal in the classroom or workspace, and precarity is produced through traditional neoliberal and social structures as well as organizational hierarchies. Privatization and living in a society that emphasizes and values the individual has removed many public social safety nets, further contributing to and enhancing the economic precarity of many BIPOC. Beginning most aggressively with the Reagan presidency, the economic model of neo-liberalism has been characterized by and resulted in a new gilded age of ever-expanding wealth inequality. While these policies are race evasive, BIPOC have been affected the most as they suffered from residential segregation, mass incarceration and countless other covert and overt racist policy. Today, economic precarity inhibits many people's opportunities and methods to disrupting and I validate this precarity by discussing different forms that positive disruption may take in the classroom and in the organizational space. Due in part to an individuals' felt and real precarity, one form of disruption may be preferred over the other. The lack of safety net and government public supports means that, especially in the workforce, people will tolerate much more abuse and trauma than they are comfortable with simply because they cannot afford to lose a job. Providing different methods to positive disruption should hopefully allow people to mitigate and diminish any trauma they are or have experienced. As will be discussed, it will be important to combine practices of disruption with those of inclusion to be able to increase the breadth and depth of the organizational change desired. I encourage you to hold onto these concepts and your purpose as a social worker and leader as you read, reflect and engage with the chapters and discussion questions.

Chapter Outlines

I begin this project by defining what it means to locate ourselves by identifying and naming our histories, our identities and our traumas and how that identifying and naming is subject to change based on the social and political context. How we locate ourselves is a fluid process that is subject to change as we grow. I define the practice principle of being able to locate ourselves as consistent and intentional reflection and self-interrogation. As social workers, this process is even more important because we work with and for people, organizations and communities trying to help them overcome obstacles within deeply embedded structural inequalities. The ways in which we understand our client's histories and identities, the interventions we use, the theories that ground us, the research we take part in, and how we lead are all impacted by our social location. We locate ourselves to identify and name our lens, and identifying our lens is important because it is the way that we "see" and relate to the professor, the client, the community, the organization and the research.

In this project, I use myself and my own narratives of locating myself in an effort to model the fluidity as well as the challenges that accompany this process. I introduce the theoretical framework and practice principle of positive disruption through the use of my personal narrative. Positive disruption is defined as an inclusive framework that is used to "enter" spaces that are white and normative, both in body and in ideology. "Enter" meaning to honor the skill of curiosity to question the normative teachings, unpack rhetoric and suggest a more inclusive and trauma-informed way of being and leading. Positive disruption involves a certain level of vulnerability because you are questioning beliefs and practices and disrupting the status quo. There is an inherent precariousness to this. In this process you are also making yourself more visible to others and ideally, the courage and vulnerability you model gives permission for others to do the same.

Throughout this book I use the language of Black, Indigenous and people of color to include the diversity of identity among non-white groups. At times, I will shorten this and use the acronym BIPOC. I will also use the descriptors of Black and Brown bodies. My intentionality around language is to be inclusive for how people identify, which is in many diverse ways. While I hold the experiences of people of color central in this project, I remain aware of anti-Black sentiment that lives in the bodies of dark-skinned people and disrupts all categories of identity, across and within culture.

In Chapter 1, I present, define, unpack and reconceptualize certain terms that are normalized in the field of social work; cultural competency, leadership, trauma and trauma-informed practice. This unpacking and re-definition of foundational terms will be crucial to the understanding of this project moving forward. I share my narratives because my personal and professional stories intersect with all of these terms and how I have tried to positively disrupt the white and normative spaces these terms and practices define and occupy. I also share that in some instances, I had to relinquish leadership roles because I did not want to just embody diversity, but instead work and lead in a culture that was equitable and inclusive. Within these stories we see the intersections of trauma and leadership.

Chapter 2 moves us to a more explicit discussion of trauma-informed practice as an ideology that is ripe for inclusion. Yet, trauma-informed practice as it stands now needs to be re-thought. The core principles of safety, choice, collaboration, trustworthiness and empowerment do not alone account for an integration of diversity, equity and inclusion. We see how organizations are either driven toward a trauma-informed mission or a diversity, equity and inclusion mission. My hope is to create a truly inclusive organizational culture that is able to live in both spaces simultaneously.

In Chapter 3, I unpack leadership in social work, questioning the inclusivity of the social work field particularly for Black, Indigenous and people of color. In this chapter I interrogate the terms "safety" and "authenticity," terms that are buzz words used to describe ways of leading that present a false sense and impossible picture of being and leading.

In Chapter 4, I define transformational leadership as a framework for social work practice and social work leadership. Transformational leadership in my practice is trauma-informed social work practice through the lens of diversity and inclusion. That is, a re-conceptualization of specific terms to aid in the efforts toward social justice, that begins with the self. In this chapter I identify eight traits and tools of transformational leadership. These eight traits and tools are; mindfulness, compassion, comfort with nuance, courage, vulnerability, empathic accountability, curiosity and being trauma responsive.

In Chapter 5, I provide the reader with the opportunity to reflect on the previous chapter. Specifically, I ask the reader to channel their own experiences, behaviors and choices in relation to how we would expect a transformational leader to model leadership. Following this, I return to a discussion on opportunities for disruption and then discuss personal and professional challenges that work to potentially inhibit our ability to lead from a transformational lens.

In Chapter 6, we "Envision a New." I begin this chapter with hope and possibility. In this chapter I revisit the social work mission of social justice and the explicit connection to positive disruption as an agent of change that upholds that mission. Part of the process of envisioning a new begins with the recognition of where the reader is in mind and heart space at the culmination of this book, and how they plan to operationalize the skills and lessons learned in their personal and professional life. The chapter then transitions to sample workshops and case studies.

The book's formal end recognizes and acknowledges that this work begins at home. The end of this reading truly marks the beginning of our journey. As the writer, my only hope is that you leave this book more self-aware and open to vulnerability than you entered it, and that you employ this newfound vulnerability and propensity to disrupt in creating more just and inclusive futures.

Each chapter begins with the practice of locating yourself and concludes with discussion questions for you to work alone or in small groups as a way to digest, internalize and operationalize the material that was just presented. Finally, throughout all six chapters I use the real-life and extreme example of the COVID-19 pandemic and the public outrage that ensued following the murders of Ahmaud Arbery, Breonna Taylor and George Floyd to illustrate the importance of incorporating diversity and inclusion into trauma-informed social work practice and leadership. As I continue to write, we are still in this pandemic, racial trauma is visceral, and each day that goes by I am reminded of the opportunity of new transformational leadership. Every day we see examples of leadership that is neurotic and driven by privilege, ego and fear rather than by love, compassion and empathic accountability.

Guide to Reading This Book

As you begin to read, I encourage you to:

1. Locate yourselves in the here and now. What are the facets of your identity? What are your identities of privilege and of oppression?
2. Intentionally reflect on and write about the points of positive disruptions you have experienced in your life.
3. Intentionally name the impetus for this each disruption and write down how that felt.
4. Intentionally reflect and share examples of how your inclusion or presence in one space has allowed the people you are with to conflate, ignore and openly exclude people who share other facts of your identity.
5. Intentionally think about how you have defined trauma and what else could you include in this definition.
6. Intentionally reflect on and write about your understanding and internalization of diversity and inclusion. Where do you feel challenged in this space?
7. Finally, as I tell my students, take notes, write in the margins and feel free to send me comments following each chapter or the whole read. I hope to introduce both nuance and understanding of the self in the quest for truly inclusive spaces.

Note

1. Precarity is defined by Butler as, "the politically induced condition in which certain populations suffer from failing social and economic networks.... becoming differentially exposed to injury, violence, death." (Butler 2009, 25).

References

Anzaldua, G. (1987). *Borderlands/La frontera: The New mestiza*. Iowa City, IA: Aunt Lute Books.

Bryant, H. (2018). *The heritage: Black athletes, a divided America, and the politics of patriotism*. Boston, MA: Beacon Press.

Butler, J. (2015). *Notes toward a performative theory of assembly*. London, UK: Harvard University Press.

DiAngelo, R. (2018). *White fragility*. Boston, MA: Beacon Press.

Gassam, J. (2019, December 29). Your unconscious bias trainings keep failing because You're not addressing systemic bias. *Forbes*. Available at https://www.forbes.com/sites/janicegassam/2020/12/29/your-unconscious-bias-trainings-keep-failing-because-youre-not-addressing-systemic-bias/#486ed9f81e9d

Kapuku, R.. (2019, September 3). Why performative diversity agendas are failing the Most marginalised communities. *Medium*, p. 1. Available at https://medium.com/@reneekapuku/why-performative-diversity-agendas-are-failing-the-most-marginalised-communities-aaff56024b14

Lindsey, M. (2019, July 6). *Dallas News*. Available at https://www.dallasnews.com/news/education/2019/07/06/how-this-texas-college-gives-every-single-student-help-with-trauma-mental-health/

Mbembe, A. (2019). *Necropolitics*. Durham NC: Duke University Press.

McIntosh, P. (1988). White privilege: Unpacking the invisible White knapsack. *White Privilege and Male Privilege: A Personal Account of Coming to See Correspondences Through Work in Women's*. Available at https://www.racialequitytools.org/resourcefiles/mcintosh.pdf

Menaken, R. (2017). *My grandmother's hands: Racialized trauma and the pathway to mending our hearts and bodies*. Las Vegas, NV; Central Recovery Press.

Wheeler, A. (2020, Feburary 5). 'Fake Diversity': Barnes & Noble cancels race-swapped covers. *The Guardian*.

Zelevansky, N. (2019, November 20). The big business of unconscious bias. *The New York Times*.

1

LIVED EXPERIENCE AS A TEACHING TOOL FOR DISRUPTION OF MY LENS

I vividly remember sitting in my Masters in Social Work program's human behavior course in the late 1990s. The professor was a South Asian tenured female and every human behavior theory she taught was created by a white man. I remember sitting there questioning this monolithic representation of human behavior that seemed unrelatable and inauthentic. At the same time, I recall feeling nervous to raise my hand and question her teachings. Despite the fact that critical and creative thinking were explicit learning objectives, I stayed silent due to a fear of questioning and disrupting the theoretical frameworks of white men. Not only would I have been questioning the frameworks of these white males, but by extension, that of a non-white male who was seemingly co-signing the validity of these theories. Instead what surfaced were familiar feelings of exclusion and self-doubt. My trajectory peppered with traumatic experiences and a biracial and multiethnic identity was not aligned with Erik Erikson's static states of human development. Yet, if this was the normative way of being, then how could I have the audacity to disrupt that space? After all, I was permitted entrance into this intellectual community; didn't I have to follow the normative ways of being? Student engagement does not necessarily mean curiosity is welcomed, nor was disruption of the established status quo encouraged. More so, advancement of the status quo through new inquiries was what was always expected, and discussed with most excitement.

Locating Myself

Now as a professor of social work, I start my classes with the mindset of giving students the encouragement and agency to question my teachings and my pedagogy. Permission to be curious to question is a practice in my pedagogy that is somewhat counter to what students are used to in higher education. Starting with an understanding of and engagement with their own positionalities, they interact with the theories in very diverse and nuanced ways. Essentially, I ask students to locate themselves, which means answering questions in small groups about their families of origins, their traditions, their communities, their ways of knowing and ways of learning. This practice principle of locating the self is a trauma-informed approach that incorporates the diversity and inclusion of experience into the classroom setting. Explicitly naming curiosity as a skill to be honored while locating oneself sets the foundation for our work individually and as a classroom community. This approach also is a parallel process to students' work with clients. Examples from my recent teaching in a social work research and practice doctoral course include a white and Catholic identified heterosexual female doctoral student sharing that in all her years of education, which included both a Masters in Social Work and a Law Degree, she never had a professor ask her to bring her whole self into the classroom and engage with the theories through the lens of her positionality. Similarly, a Chinese identified woman in my class during the COVID-19 pandemic, was fraught with anxiety about her family in China and remained consumed with the dangers of the COVID-19. In this particular class, and in all my classes that I teach, the students and I spend the first class of every semester digging into this practice of self-location, and then I spend the first 10 minutes of every subsequent class allowing students to situate themselves and bring their outside lives into the classroom as part of the preparation to then learn about, question and interrogate the lessons for the day. Through this intentional and engaged pedagogy (hooks, 2010) of the self in context, we see the impact of diversity in our learning and different interpretations of theoretical frameworks. This practice innately builds community as the students share narratives of their lived experiences in the context of questioning theoretical frameworks. Classrooms become brave spaces to dialogue, empathically hold each other accountable, and positively disrupt. As a professor, this beginning exercise of locating the self is trauma-informed because of how I use myself as the instructor in the space of collaboration with the students. I share my story as they share theirs. We begin the process of developing safety within the classroom by shared vulnerability and students feel an increased sense of empowerment through the use of curiosity. Trustworthiness emerges as my pedagogy remains consistent, helping to (hopefully) diminish any felt precarity as I honor their courage for sharing and questioning. This type of leadership in the classroom allows me to be in tune with the range of potential trauma students may be experiencing outside of our classroom and how that trauma impacts the learning and my teaching. This was not the case in my personal experience as a student, the majority of my classrooms were not trauma-informed nor were they taught from an intentional pedagogical approach of inclusivity or diversity of experiences. I was not encouraged to interrogate the teachings through the lens of my nuanced positionality or my present life experiences, and I witness in my own experience with my colleagues in higher education, that this is not a normative practice in classrooms today. There is more often a disconnect between the personal life of the professor, the student and the class material. Safety is assumed, not developed or nurtured, and shared vulnerability is not practiced or valued. And yet, I would argue that the social work classroom must become another brave space of positive disruption in the effort toward the social work mission of social justice, including the sincere integration of inclusion, diversity and trauma-informed practice. I hold this quote by bell hooks close to my teaching social work practice, "classrooms cannot change if professors are unwilling to admit that to teach without biases requires that most of us learn anew, that we become students again" (hooks, 2010, p. 31). As social work educators, driven by a social justice mission, I believe there is a responsibility to model a practice of trauma-informed leadership, that is both diverse and inclusive, in the classroom and part of that practice has to hold the instructor as well as the students empathically accountable to upholding that mission.

Returning to my experience during the human behavior class in my Masters' program, I cannot remember how long I sat with those feelings of exclusion but I do know that enough of those feelings surfaced to feel that I needed to take action. My first action step was diving into literature that spoke to my experience of nuance, complexity and simultaneously building a community of solidarity. I took ownership of my education in the form of forced critical engagement and began exploring. I met women who also had biracial and multiethnic backgrounds and immersed myself in the teachings of bell hooks and Paulo Freire; two educators driven to teach by an act of love, love of humanity, inclusion and diversity. I found an intersection between the exclusion of my experiences and the teachings of those who focused on engaged pedagogy grounded in the theoretical framework of connection, belonging and love. "In Freire's world, to be passionate and to love in the midst of all our fears, anxieties, and imperfections truly constituted powerful expressions of our humanity – the humanity we had courageously embrace as educators committed to the practice of freedom," (Darder, 2002, p. 40). I interpret this quote to mean, freedom from our own, often times traumatic, narratives in order to sincerely enter into the lives of others, such as students and clients. As a social work educator, I am in a constant state of readjustment because I bend my knowledge to the lives of my students in the classroom and teach not as an expert, but as a guide and a learner. I am grounded in my own narrative but not in reverence to it. The literature of critical educators, many of whom I reference throughout this book, served as a way to normalize my experiences outside of the dominate discourses being taught and also as a way to approach my family and the world from a healing place of love. I have always been led by my heart and in some instances, this was not the most balanced way and at the same time, it was the only way I know to both work and heal.

In thinking through the importance of teaching social work students to honor curiosity and adopt a critical analysis, I am reminded of a Black female doctoral student I am advising. During the preparation of her dissertation proposal, we had a conversation about her dissertation which focuses on the lived experiences of Black social work supervisors within the supervisory relationship. Upon review, she discovered many gaps in the supervisory literature including a dearth of information related specifically to the experience of Black social work supervisors within the supervisory relationship. When it came to the part of the literature review that required her to take a critical look at the social work profession, and specifically supervision, her response to me was, "who am I to critique this profession?" Despite the fact that as a Black woman supervisor herself, she was able to recall countless examples of exclusion from the very same professionals who also occupied a supervisory role. Even as someone who has chosen to spend significant time and money uplifting the voices of Black social work supervisors by obtaining her PhD, she remained disconnected from the literature and her lived experience, as if her lived experience had to fit into the dominant discourse. To leave out her lived experiences of exclusion would be to flatten her experiences, minimize the impact of the racism she experienced, and uphold the white and normative status quo. Social workers must notice the moments when we can shift our clinical lens to see something deeper and more complex than the picture that is being presented. For me it was a feeling, a visceral response to the traditional social work material that was being taught and the lack of space to dialogue in a sincere way about who and what is being excluded from the discourse, despite the social justice mandate of the profession.

I feel it today. I now look to my physical reactions as signs of the trauma of exclusion as well as when I need to positively disrupt a conversation, be it a classroom discussion, faculty meeting, a committee meeting or a coaching session with a CEO. My palms begin to sweat, my stomach turns and I start to physically shift in my seat. I watch and listen to my body (Menakem, 2017). These physical reactions, perhaps post-trauma reactions, are the manifestation of felt trauma of entering a space that feels exclusive and invalidating. The felt fear of speaking up, claiming my voice and space in the conversation. These reactions happen less in individual coaching sessions, especially when I am working with Black people and people of color. They happen more in the predominantly white university space. At the same time, I use these physical reactions as signs of the intentional mindfulness that is required for positive disruption. The disruption eases the physical manifestations of trauma. It is in fact a mind, body and spiritual experience. These are the moments when I feel my body in alignment with my mind. I enter dialogues with courage and vulnerability without expectation because I also know I could be put back in the box or even worse, dismissed. In many ways, entering that space is healing because once I speak and share, the physical manifestations of previous traumas subside, at least for that moment.

Social workers, our lens has great potential to evolve. Think about your purpose for obtaining a Masters in Social Work. What brought you to the social work field and what is the lens from which you view the social work profession from? I'd like for you to take a few moments to answer those questions, whether it be in the margins or through a different mode. The next part of this chapter is devoted to defining the terms like leadership, trauma, diversity and inclusion through the lens of the dominant discourse. We have begun to find points of contention, disruption in an effort to introduce nuance, ambivalence and ultimately upset the status quo.

Disrupting Common Definitions

Cultural Competency

Traditional definitions of cultural competency define this concept and practice model as a static state, as something that is achievable. Social work has struggled, and continues to do so, with implementing institutional and systemic analyses of racism, whiteness, and racial power within its practice, education, and research settings. This is despite the fact that one of the distinguishing features of social work is its focus on the environment (Quiros, Varghese, & Vanidestine, 2020). The mandate within the social service world is social justice. Yet, because social justice is often framed within the context of "cultural competency" and thus is focused on categories of culture and ethnicity, it leads to implicitly endorsing a color-blind framework by de-emphasizing the significance of "race", racism, and conflating identity (Abrams & Moio, 2009; Bonilla-Silva, 2010; Schiele, 2007; Yee, 2005). For example, social workers who rely on the cultural competency model to understand "race" may focus at the micro level to understand how people are "culturally different" in lieu of understanding how categories of race result in differential social power (Varghese, 2016). A critical observer must ask, "different from whom?" In most cases, the answer is people identified as white, who are often "unmarked" or not "raced" yet receive unearned social, economic and psychological advantages in the racial hierarchy in the United States. As a graduate student I vividly remember those paragraphs titled "African Americans," "Latinos," and "Asians," that were required reading meant to fulfill the culturally competence mandate of the profession. Somehow it was expected that reading what are conflated notions of stereotyped identities and memorizing a set of academic and interpersonal skills would equip students with the skills needed to work with non-white populations. As a woman of color and budding social worker reading these passages, I recall all the questions I had. The questions ranged from self-doubt, because there was never a passage on being biracial or bicultural, to confusion because I knew that the Black Diaspora was more than just the African American experience. African American is not synonymous with Black, just as I was familiar with the diversity and nuance within the Latinx culture.

Understanding "white culture," white ideology and the social power manifested in whiteness are not usually examined within the context of cultural competency (Quiros, Varghese, & Vanidestine, 2020). Furthermore, discussions solely focused on "race" and racism often imply relevance exclusively to Black, Indigenous and people of color (BIPOC) while excluding an analysis of whiteness. This can narrowly frame BIPOC as the primary location for challenging racial injustices without questioning the dominant white ideology that created the racism and continues to underpin and perpetuate the racism and trauma experienced by BIPOC within universities and organizations today. BIPOC is an acronym that stands for Black, Indigenous, people of color that was crafted in 2013 but became more prevalent and popularized on the internet in the aftermath of the killing of George Floyd. Positively disrupting the notion of "cultural competence" is required to bridge the gap between micro and macro practice and to look more deeply and properly at trauma, inclusion and diversity within the field of social work. This disruption is necessary to help students in the very beginning of their education engage in a more nuanced and critical understanding and analysis of the trauma of the institutionalized racial hierarchy within the United States. This should be embedded throughout the social work curriculum and integrated into field education. Without doing so, social work students remain ill equipped to engage in critical discussions about race and whiteness in the classroom and in their work with clients, groups and communities.

Positive Disruption: Example from a Colleague in the Classroom

A white and cisgender male colleague of mine has spent his career understanding and interrogating his whiteness. His name is Dr. Todd Vanidestine. We worked together at Adelphi University, facilitated classroom dialogues and delivered several trainings on Whiteness. In trainings, we co-facilitate and use our identities as a model for social work practice, specifically engaging across race and gender differences. It is always so interesting to see how participants respond to us based on our identities. For example, he is usually the one to be referred to as Dr. or Professor whereas I am referred to by my first name. For this project I asked him to share how he engages students in his classroom beyond the cultural competency framework. He shared this:

> As I walk into a classroom full of people, many of whom I don't know, I know that everyone in the room will immediately make assumptions about me. Two of the most prominent physical characteristics are the

color of my skin (white) and presenting gender (cisgender male), which are inherently related to positions of social power in our society. For the purpose of this case example, I will focus on techniques on how to examine and disrupt whiteness in the classroom and beyond. First of all, it's imperative to create supportive spaces, such as a classroom learning community, where we can critically examine our identities and their relationship to privileging processes (relatively more social power) and marginalizing processes (relatively less social power). Given that social power is a part of each process, I ask the students about it. What power do I have as a professor? What power do they have as a group of students? What power do they have as an individual? How can they use their power to change unjust conditions? I acknowledge the inherent power of my position, and institutional policies that exert power over me, in a way that embraces a commitment to analyzing power as a method for strengthening our work together. I share power by asking them what their expectations are of me as a professor, which I list on the board and encourage follow-up at any time during the semester when I'm not fulfilling those obligations. Additionally, we examine how social power imbalances and injustices affect individual students, their campus community, and their society as manifested in racism (white supremacy), sexism, heterosexism, classism, ableism, and other forms of discrimination.

After discussing the power imbalances among various identities, I ask the class which of the above "-isms" are difficult to discuss with your family, friends, colleagues or people they serve in the community. Students will often provide various answers and I allow this to continue for a few minutes. Sometimes racism (and white supremacy to a lesser extent) is mentioned. Most of the time students will only mention the "-ism" without discussing "why" the concept is difficult for them to discuss. Regardless of whether racism or white supremacy are discussed by the students, I start explaining my relationship to whiteness and racism, and the connection to racialized power embedded into the fabric of our country, society, institutions and communities. After sharing my personal challenges with examining racism and white supremacy, I ask the entire class what their thoughts are regarding these concepts. During these initial discussions, they listen to their colleagues' experiences and this becomes the foundation for students to more thoroughly examine their own racialization. Discussing social power as it relates to racism and white supremacy early in the semester begins an ongoing commitment to critically reflect on both our dominant and subordinate positions in society. As relationships build within the learning community, the various layers of racism and white supremacy emerge by incorporating real-time examples such as the current social justice activism associated with George Floyd's murder.

Positive Disruption in My Scholarship

As I write this project, I have come to the realization that my 2009 dissertation titled "The Social Construction of Racial and Ethnic Identity Among Women of Color from Mixed Ancestry: Psychological Freedoms and Sociological Constraints," was an early attempt to positively disrupt labels assigned to identity and the notion of "cultural competence." I share in my autobiographical statement at the conclusion of the dissertation, "my personal biography influenced the desire to investigate women from mixed heritages." I quote Denzin & Lincoln (1994), "every researcher speaks from within a distinct interpretive community that configures, in its special way, the multicultural, gendered components of the research art" (p. 30). My research art was, and remains, a qualitative inquiry of positive disruption in an attempt to make room for the enduring complexity of the human condition and use that data, and myself, to create spaces that are inclusive and diverse. My identity and methods as a qualitative researcher are not separate from how I teach and consult. In both spaces I rely on building relationships, collecting stories, staying with curiosity that drives the inquiry and pulling together emergent themes – somewhat similar to a documentary filmmaker. In all spaces I am very alert to what is unfolding and the spontaneous probes enabling me to explore more deeply. My attempts at positive disruption can also be found throughout my other scholarship. I share an excerpt below from a 2012 paper (Quiros, 2012) about the impact of identity conflation on the classroom setting:

> Despite the saliency of cultural and national identity, women who locate themselves as having both a Black racial identity and a cultural identity are silenced by the limited and fixed constructions of race. The term Black is used to describe a universal set of social experiences,

thereby reducing identity to one's perceived race and assuming a commonality of experience based on appearance. For example, there is no room for I am Black and Jamaican, I am Black and Puerto Rican, I am Black and Jewish. As a result, there is a lack of understanding of changing subjectivities and individual agency. These attributions of perceived and diminished identity become problematic because the complexity of the individual's experience is conflated. Individuals with a Black and ethnic identification are unable to operate with their fluid and dynamic identities because of the narrowness of race in the American context, and there are consequences to this constriction. When one's personal cultural identification is not recognized, validated, and legitimized by others, one may never feel fully "authenticated" (King & DaCosta, 1996). That is, when an aspect of the self goes unrecognized it is almost as if that part of the person ceases to exist. Combating invisibility, marginalization and the stagnation of identity is a struggle. Black ethnic women must contend with every day. How does this play out within the classroom setting? As educators, how do we elevate the voices of students who belie traditional racial and cultural categories thereby creating a safe space for them to be fully seen and heard?

Leadership

The literature on leadership is no exception, and is primarily from a white, cisgender and male lens (Sanchez-Hucles & Davis, 2010). This means that a monolithic representation of leadership becomes normalized (Liu & Baker, 2016) and the impact is the exclusion of the experiences of women and mostly leaders of color (Hite, 2007; Patton & Haynes, 2014; Sanchez-Hucles & Davis, 2010). Unpacking the intersectionality of gender and race, there is racial comfortability among white leaders. Leaders do not have to think about their whiteness because the space is predominantly white (Lowe, 2013). Women leaders of color are at a significant disadvantage achieving representation in leadership positions in the academy and in organizations (Carli & Eagly, 2016; Chin & Sanchez-Hucles, 2007; Festekjian, Tram, Murray, Sy, & Huynh, 2014; Gündemir, Homan, de Dreu, & van Vugt, 2014; Warner, Ellmann, & Boesch, 2018).

I think of student learning in the classroom on micro, meso and macro levels. Is there an explicit acknowledgement of the origins of the leadership theory being from a white, cisgender and male perspective? I think of the experiences that leaders of color face. I sat on the committee of a doctoral student whose qualitative dissertation addressed this gap in the literature; the experiences of Black males in nonprofit leadership. Dr. Damyn Kelly, a Black, cisgender and male CEO himself included an Addendum about his own personal journey. He writes:

This study and its subject matter are one that is truly personal to this researcher. For I meet all the inclusion criteria required for the study. The study was also personal as I have often struggled with the question, why am I the only Black male in the room or oftentimes, why am I the only Black person in the room. What made me special? What privileges did I receive that allowed me to have served as a chief executive of several human service not for profit organization over the course of more than twenty years. What led to me being recruited for three of those positions. "Was I different, was it me or more importantly; what made me special?" The motivation for this study and my pursuit of a Doctorate degree was in fact a search to answers for those questions.

The normalization of Whiteness in so many leadership theoretical frameworks begs the question of what happened to the awareness of the inclusion of Black, Indigenous and people of color and the value of that diversity? The racial hierarchy is evident in these spaces as we see little racial and gender diversity in executive leadership. Whiteness is affirmed and maintained. Having served for a short time in an Associate Dean position I was familiar with the feelings of isolation and dissonance and the sea of whiteness that surrounds leadership (Ahmed, 2012). I have stepped away from and turned down opportunities for traditional leadership positions in the academy and elsewhere because of the isolation and dissonance that Sara Ahmed writes about. These traditional leadership roles do not feel like positions able to positively disrupt or be an agent of change but rather ways to provide an institution with diversity through my body. Positions that fill the diversity quota in the performative sense we discussed earlier. As scholar Sara Ahmed states, "diversity becomes about changing the perceptions of whiteness rather than changing the whiteness of organizations. Changing perceptions of whiteness can be how an institution can reproduce whiteness, as that which exists but is no longer perceived" (Ahmed, 2012). At this point in my career, I am interested in an inquiry and complex analysis of how social workers and leaders participate in the construction of their world, and how this in turn shapes the ways they see themselves and are seen and experienced by others whom they serve. Beliefs and mindsets of leaders in all spaces are paramount in transitioning from the dominant, white, male and positivistic organizational cultures to transformative, compassionate and sincere spaces (Carter, Mossholder, Feild, & Armenakis, 2014). I see these transformative spaces lead by critical and transformational leaders who use themselves and their vision to positively disrupt, and through relationship building coupled with vulnerability, create spaces of inclusion and diversity that are trauma-informed. We will cover the specifics of this in a later chapter called Transformational Leadership.

Positive Disruption

Another attempt at disruption within the leadership space with the goal of inclusion, equity and diversity came two years later at a conference focused on academically based community organizing. The conference began with a panel of University leaders and their narratives on the ways that each university was engaging with communities of color. After the panel I hesitantly raised my hand and asked the leaders on the panel, all of whom were Presidents, Chancellors and Provosts of Universities, if there was work done before hand on insider–outsider positionality. More specifically if they, and faculty involved with the projects, had spent any time reflecting on their positionalities as white leaders in the academy, and the ways in which they may uphold beliefs and values of institutional whiteness (Ahmed, 2012) and what impact this may have had on the culture they help to create in the university and the communities they were working with. The room first fell silent and then I was met with defensive responses from the panel and what felt like shock that such a question would even be asked. They had not. Using my social work person in environment lens, I was asking the panelists obvious questions. I had participants of color approach me later, thanking me for the question and what they called my "courage;" courage to notice and question unexamined whiteness and how it lives in the organizations. What was significant about this moment was first, the normalization of whiteness from very high levels of leadership and second, the private comments I received afterward. Returning to the notion of precarity, we see how felt precarity surfaces when whiteness is verbally noticed or called into question. The leadership literature does not ask that leaders locate themselves in an effort to understand their personal engagements with upholding a racial hierarchy in the leadership space. A racial hierarchy that is inherently traumatic for and to non-white communities of people. Without first locating oneself, the attempts to make room for diversity and inclusion fall flat. Second, what stops Black, Indigenous and people of color from asking critical questions about whiteness? I desire for a normalization of the challenging of the status quo and the very obvious disruption of all white bodies who occupy these positions. At the same time, I am reminded of the psychological labor of Black, Indigenous and people of color in those moments to notice the "gap" and ask the questions in an effort not to call anyone out, but to make room, share space, notice and dialogue, and find ways to be inclusive.

Trauma

Now we come to the intersection with Trauma. Traumatic experiences are inherently complex, unpredictable and involve a loss of control. Judith Herman's (1997) ground breaking work taught us that, "traumatic events are extraordinary, not because they occur rarely, but rather because they overwhelm the ordinary human adaptations to life." Herman (1997) also emphasized that the foundation of all trauma work is safety; physical, emotional and spiritual safety. The premise being that before clients delve into their histories and narratives of the traumatic event(s), a level of safety within the therapeutic alliance should be achieved first. This presents a challenge for clients of color whose histories are also grounded in racial trauma. We see the complexity of social workers working with clients who have histories of interpersonal traumas coupled with the inherent racial trauma of living in the United States. If social workers do not have the self-awareness and tools to comprehensively understand the importance of thinking about race and racism and engaging in sincere discussions of race and racism, how do social workers help clients seek safety in the therapeutic alliance? How social workers use themselves as a tool to help to increase the felt safety in the individual therapeutic alliance and in group work, specifically when working with trauma, is important. Traits such as vulnerability, mindfulness, curiosity, and understanding the nuance and complexity of race will help to increase the felt sense of safety in the alliance. Additionally, when working across racial differences, if race and the subsequent racial trauma become invisible then whiteness and the power manifested in whiteness is affirmed and maintained.

Furthermore, the initial step of seeking safety often presents a challenge for beginning social work clinicians who are hungry for immediate connection with their clients and gain a certain level of satisfaction and validation from client's disclosure of their trauma histories in the first or second session. The value and importance of seeking this safety in individual work first, by helping clients who have experienced trauma ground themselves and unpack the word "safety" and way of being in their treatment is critical for sustained engagement. This initial practice of seeking safety requires that the practitioner has an awareness of trauma beyond the interpersonal lens. Meaning, it requires understanding the bridge between the micro world of the client and the larger macro environment that the client lives in. Again, we revisit the person in environment framework that is central to social work practice. The practice of seeking safety also requires patience, fluidity from the social work clinician to not rush the process by looking for a quick fix, and an awareness of oneself. These practices are essential as one way to ensure that the session does not become about the clinician's needs but rather, centers the client. Not falling prey to a sense of urgency and need to diagnose is crucial in being able to develop a relationship with the client beyond a diagnosis. I see students in the courses I teach on trauma rush to label behaviors and assign a diagnosis gathering all the facts and listening deeply to the client in the context of their environments. This brings us, the reader, back to the earlier discussion of one's purpose in the social work field and the need to locate oneself, to first understand the clinician's interpretation of the "problem," and any triggers or implicit bias that may also be present. Moving from an unsafe world to a safe one requires collaboration and time to build trust. Even when time is limited due to the realities of managed care, it is still essential that facts are gathered and labels are not assigned based on assumptions and unchecked implicit bias.

After the initial steps of locating oneself, one way clinicians can begin this search for safety with the client is by asking clients what safety means for them and identify the "safe" people in their lives (Najavits, 2002). Working in collaboration with the client is trauma-informed and builds on the principles of trustworthiness and empowerment as the client and the clinician create a sense of shared meaning together. Doing this exercise from a lens of inclusion and diversity further deepens the relationship because the client is seen as part of larger and complex systems. In my work, the exercise of defining the word safety in collaboration with the client has worked wonders. I also have used this exercise in the classroom as a way to gauge where students sense of safety comes from and where in the environment they may feel unsafe. In addition, in the practice setting, I use the therapeutic alliance as a real-life illustration of a safe space by making session times predictable and by practicing containment and boundary setting when clients rush too not to quickly to telling it all.

Yet, there is also a consideration of intentionality to be had when using the term "safe space." Social workers also use the term "safe space" to describe the practice settings of group work, trainings and organizational settings. Instructors also use the term "safe space," in the classroom setting. However, rarely is there an intentional, mindful, permanent focus on safety in the classroom, groups, trainings or organizational climates and cultures. I struggle with the use of the term safe space in a training setting and in a classroom setting. First, I wonder if in classrooms and in interactive trainings the term "safe space" is being used in an effort to get students and participants to open up? It sounds good. The word safety has become rhetoric in the field of social work and in particular trauma and sometimes is used without an intentional guide on how to create that safe space or what that may feel like for students or participants in the group. Especially if the there is a white leader, facilitator and majority in the room. Have facilitators or leaders considered the ways that clients and students of color may not feel safe in a classroom or group setting because of their individual experiences with racism and because of systemic racism? When in a position of power, it is necessary to explicitly discuss the assumed expectation of safety as something that is problematic. Safety, in these instances, is also a temporary arrangement. While the classroom or training space may be safe while we are learning and working with clients, it wasn't safe before we were working and learning with them and it won't be tomorrow when we aren't there, so a certain censorship occurs because that safety is not permanent and therefore sentiments of constant surveillance among students and participants may exist.

While working as a social work intern serving children and adolescents in a residential facility, I witnessed this need for an intentional focus on psychological and physical safety early in my career. I observed that adolescents with substance abuse issues often relapse once they return home, despite the clinicians' best efforts. Later, working as a clinician with women who also were in recovery for "substance abuse problems," I noticed a similar trend (Savage et al., 2007). The first issue was that the clients were only receiving treatment for their substance abuse, meanwhile research tells us that the majority of clients in substance abuse programs have histories of trauma (Najavits, 2002). The dual diagnosis of Post-Traumatic Stress Disorder (PTSD) and substance abuse is incredibly common (Najavits, 2002). PTSD can be described as post trauma reactions and symptoms. Meaning, it is the reexperiencing of symptoms associated with the trauma(s) long after the trauma(s) occurred. Second, the women would enter a treatment center for a time, receive individual and group therapy, and then once they left the "Safe" group and individual spaces, they would relapse. I realized that helping clients heal is very dependent on the enactment of values of the organization and how identity is constructed and guided by context and hegemony. Collaboration, empowerment, trustworthiness, choice and safety, the tenets of trauma-informed practice, were not valued and identity was constructed and guided by a racist and reductionist mindset. More specifically, clients were not viewed holistically. The women in the treatment center, the majority of whom were women of color and labeled as "addicts," were not seen as women with histories of trauma, interpersonal trauma, institutional trauma and sociopolitical trauma. Yet, for many, the use of substances was the safest way to cope with environments fraught with racism, poverty, abuse, homelessness, neglect, single parenthood and prostitution. Many of these women were scapegoated as "non-compliant" and "resistant" by staff and administrators unwilling to reflect on how the treatment practices and overall organizational values and culture were factors in clients deemed "not ready" for treatment. The dominant narrative of the "experts" in the field prevailed without much, if any, attention paid to the possibility of opposing worldviews, differences in culture, spiritual history or practices between and among the clients, and the providers. Furthermore, providers were not asked to reflect or "locate" themselves in an effort to understand their positionality and become aware of the strategies they are imploring to "help," as well as identify any bias they may harbor about this demographic of women. Many providers from this traditional substance abuse treatment center had just graduated from the program and were confident in instituting approaches that worked for them. As a clinician working in this field, I was told more than once that I was "spoiling" the women by offering them a space to talk about their past traumas and the reasons that lead to their addictions. The universal umbrella of "Recovery" made it easy to conflate identity and minimize differences in culture, race and the impacts of structural racism and sexism. The White and Eurocentric values of recovery called into question the legitimacy of the salience of identity for women of color and had a direct impact on their self-perception. My earliest experiences before and during my Masters' program were foundational to understanding the intersections of trauma, identity construction and inclusion.

Through my studies and life experiences I began to better understand how trauma is intrinsically and systematically linked to experiences of racism, sexism, classism, ethno-religious oppression and homophobia, and its impact on identity construction. Therefore, the field cannot be race evasive. I saw this void of intersection in the field beginning as a student and continuing as clinician, researcher, administrator and faculty member. In 2013, my colleague, Dr. Roni Berger, and I wrote an article called *Responding to the Sociopolitical Complexity of Trauma: An Integration of Theory and Practice.* The impetus for this article was to address a gap in the trauma literature, and integrate the political and the intersectionality of traditionally marginalized communities. We used postmodern feminist theory to disrupt the traditional trauma space and offered tools for practice. I have found that postmodern approaches, in general, are a response to normative social work practice theories and interventions that disrupt the status quo. In this case, positioning postmodern feminism as the standpoint theory gave voice to the intersectionality of gender, race, and class and lent credence to how women's socio-cultural position interacts with the other aforementioned systems of power and oppression to determine making meaning of their lived experiences. From the research we did in writing this paper we discovered the work of Burstow (2003), who also positively disrupted the trauma space with her article titled; *Toward a Radical Understanding of Trauma and Trauma Work.* I still support this definition of trauma, "a reaction to a kind of wound. It is a reaction to profoundly injurious events and situations in the real world and, indeed, to a world in which people are routinely wounded" (Burstow, 2003, p. 1302). It is the social workers' responsibility to tend to every aspect of the metaphorical wound, especially the wounds that feel most uncomfortable and difficult to tackle, such as the wounds of interpersonal and systemic racism. Thus, traumatizing socio-political circumstances must be part of the understanding and addressing of people's psychosocial problems (Quiros & Berger, 2013).

The Precariousness of Disruption: The Intersections of Trauma and Leadership

I took my sabbatical the semester after my time serving as the Associate Dean. It was not until I was physically and mentally away from campus that I realized how my behaviors prior to my sabbatical were manifestations of the trauma I experienced in that leadership position. Months before my sabbatical was granted the school became an increasingly unsafe and unpredictable place for me. I became hypervigilant and experienced a loss of internal control. I would sit in my car for an extended period of time before putting on my psychological armor to enter the school. Even worse I lost my drive to subsequently become a Dean one day. I spent time journaling on my experiences and, as a qualitative researcher, couched them thematically; lack of mentorship, exclusion, pay inequity, racism and sexism. During this journaling process I also came to the harsh realization that I had served as an invisible coach, unknowingly. My role as Associate Dean was more like a coach to the Dean around his issues of white privilege and white fragility, and less as a leader of his administration. I was asked to guide him behind the scenes yet shunned when I tried to use my own voice in speaking up against overt racism and collusion in the institution. Once, in an attempt to assist faculty and administration with a student issue, I was told the by the other Associate Dean, "you speak with too much authority" and in the same conversation, "you think you are a knight in shining armor trying to save people." It became apparent that positively disrupting power relations, and exposing a deficiency of other faculty and administration in understanding and dealing with race and trauma, led to personal animosity between them and me. I was not supported in this space, with the exception of my few colleagues who became close friends. The animosity was a result of their feelings of exclusion, lack of understanding, inability and investment in a white, and patriarchal system, all of which were never formally acknowledged between us.

For the person who experiences trauma the world becomes an increasingly unsafe place. Not only are you battling the internal post trauma reactions, you are also battling whether or not you want to do anything or say something about said trauma. For a while my complacency to silence had to do with questioning whether or not these acts were a figment of my imagination or wondering if I was making a bigger deal of them then they deserved. Despite my education, the stereotype of the overly emotional and dramatic Latina played mind tricks on me. Here lies the intersection of trauma and racial and cultural identity. If I were a white woman, perhaps I would have felt that I had more authority to speak up and also that I would be believed. Simultaneous gender and racial discrimination carry different baggage than gender discrimination alone. There becomes a decision of whether or not to remain silent, seek help or speak up with the risk of exposure and exclusion in the best case, and persecution in the worst case. These decisions are heavily impacted by race, culture, gender and the intersectionality of all of that (Crenshaw, 1989). While being trained by Dr. Lisa Najavits, the author of *Seeking Safety* (Najavits, 2002), early in my trajectory, I learned a great deal about the unexplainable psychological harm that is caused by trauma and the subsequent self and societal compassion that is needed to heal. I also came to understand the resiliency involved in healing and the agency in using trauma and this trauma in particular, as an opportunity for self-growth and personal affirmation. Even now, when I share my stories of my former experience in higher education leadership, when I get to the part of why I stepped down, my voice quivers a little and in the back of my mind I still question if my audience actually believes what I am saying.

There is trauma and emotional labor in positive disruption. I stand by the notion that only a few of those students and social workers trained in trauma work have been taught the skills to locate themselves in order to engage constructively across and within racial divides. Specifically, the skills I am referring to are the recognition and ability to name racism, white supremacy and systemic inequalities as traumas and include them as central components to the work with clients. Few social workers educators teach the skills to push back against offensive statements and grasp and internalize the real concerns and danger that Black students and Black clients live with every day. As a result of this gap in service delivery, the experiences of students and leaders of color in universities and organizations impacted by the structural racism are excluded from the trauma narrative. There are the experiences of trauma and then there are the attempts at shutting down the disruption to uphold, support the status quo and stay comfortable. Embedded within a trauma-informed leadership model from a diversity and inclusion lens, is locating yourself and identifying trauma and the creation of trauma-informed and trauma responsive systems of leadership that consider the complexity of trauma among non-dominant staff and clients within organizations; all leading to comprehensive ways of leading that furthers missions of diversity, equity and inclusion, and social justice.

Discussion Questions

1. What were your general reactions to this chapter?
2. Locate yourself by answering these questions alone or in small groups:

    a. Where did you grow up and how diverse was it?
    b. What were your memories with your socio-economic background?
    c. Where did you have privilege?
    d. What messages did you receive from your family, friends and community about groups who were different than yours?

3. What are your lived experiences that inform your entry into the social work profession?
4. What lived experiences inform your work in the social work profession?
5. How have you used these experiences as tools for your practice? If you have not used your lived experiences as tools for practice, where do you imagine you would use them as tools for practice?
6. Can you reflect on or identify any experiences where you have been told stories that restrict/confuse who you are or your sense of self?

7. How important is it for you to stay comfortable at the expense of others?

References

Abrams, L. S., & Moio, J. A. (2009). Critical race theory and the cultural competence dilemma in social work education. *Journal of Social Work Education*, *45*(2), 245–261.

Ahmed, S. (2012). *On being included: Racism and diversity in institutional life*. London, UK: Duke University Press.

Bonilla-Silva, E. (2010). *Racism without racists: Color-blind racism and racial inequality in contemporary America*. Lanham, MD: Rowman & Littlefield.

Burstow, B. (2003). Toward a radical understanding of trauma and trauma work. *Violence against Women*, *9*(11), 1293–1317.

Carli, L. L., & Eagly, A. H. (2016). Women face a labyrinth: An examination of metaphors for women leaders. *Gender in Management: An International Journal*, *31*(8), 514–527.

Carter, M. Z., Mossholder, K. W., Feild, H. S., & Armenakis, A. A. (2014). Transformational leadership, interactional justice, and organizational citizenship behavior: The effects of racial and gender dissimilarity between supervisors and subordinates. *Group & Organizational Management*, *39*(6), 691–719.

Chin, J. L., & Sanchez-Hucles, J. (2007). Diversity and leadership. *American Psychologist, 62(6)*, 608–609.

Darder, A. (2002). *Reinventing Paulo Freire: A pedagogy of love*. Cambridge, MA: The Perseus Books.

Denzin, N. K., & Lincoln, Y. S. (Eds.). (1994). *Handbook of qualitative research*. Thousand Oaks, CA: Sage Publications.

Festekjian, A., Tram, S., Murray, C. B., Sy, T., & Huynh, H. P. (2014). I see me the way you see me: The influence of race on interpersonal and intrapersonal leadership perceptions. *Journal of Leadership and Organizational Study, 21(1)*, 102–119.

Gündemir, S., Homan, A. C., De Dreu, C. K. W., & van Vugt, M. (2014). Think leader, think white? Capturing and weakening an implicit pro-white leadership bias. *PLoS One*, *9*(1), e83915.

Herman, J. (1997). *Trauma and recovery*. New York: Basic Books.

Hite, L. M. (2007). Hispanic women managers and professionals: Reflections on life and work. *Gender, Work & Organization, 14*(1), 20–36.

hooks, b. (2010). *Teaching critical thinking.* New York, NY: Routledge.

King, R. C., & DaCosta, K. (1996). Changing face, changing race: The remaking of race in Japanese, American and African American communities. In M. P.P. Root (Ed.), *The multiracial experience: Racial borders as the new frontier* (pp. 227–244). Newbury Park, CA: Sage Publications.

Liu, H., & Baker, C. (2016). White Knights: Leadership as the heroicisation of whiteness. *Leadership, 12*(4), 420–448.

Lowe, F. (2013). Keeping leadership White: Invisible blocks to Black leadership and its denial in White organizations. *Journal of Social Work Practice, 27*(2), 149–162.

Menaken, R. (2017). *My Grandmother's hands: Racialized trauma and the pathway to mending our hearts and bodies.* Las Vegas, NV: Central Recovery Press.

Najavits, L. (2002). *Seeking safety: A treatment manual for PTSD and substance abuse.* New York, NY: Guildford Press.

Patton, L. D., & Haynes, C. M. (2014; 2013). Using critical interpretive lenses to examine glass ceiling effects through qualitative research. *New Directions for Institutional Research, 2013*(159), 25–35.

Quiros, L. (2012). Raising the voice: Teaching through a multicultural lens. *Journal of Teaching in Social Work, 32*(5), 518–531.

Quiros, L., & Berger, R. (2013). Responding to the sociopolitical complexity of trauma: An Integration of Theory and Practice. *Journal of Loss and Trauma: International Perspectives on Stress & Coping, 20*(2),149–159.

Quiros, L., Varghese, R., & Vanidestine, T. (2020). Disrupting the single story: Challenging dominant trauma narratives through a critical race lens. *Traumatology, 26*(2), 160–168.

Sanchez-Hucles, J. V., & Davis, D. D. (2010). Women and women of Color in leadership: Complexity, *identity, and intersectionality. American Psychologist, 65*(3), 171–181.

Savage, A., Quiros, L., Dodd, S. J. & Bonavota, D. (2007). Building trauma informed practice: Appreciating the impact of trauma in the lives of women with substance abuse and mental health problems. *Journal of Social Work Practice in the Addictions, 7*(1-2), 91–116.

Schiele, J. H. (2007). Implications of the equality-of-oppressions paradigm for curriculum content on BIPOC. *Journal of Social Work Education, 43*(1), 83–100.

Yee, J. Y. (2005). Critical anti-racism praxis: The concept of Whiteness implicated. In S. Hicks, J. Fook, & R. Pozzuto (Eds.), *Social work: A critical turn* (pp. 87–103). Toronto, Ontario, Canada: Thompson Educational Publishing.

Varghese, R. (2016). Teaching to transform: Addressing race and racism in the teaching of clinical social work practice. *Journal for Social Work Education*, 52, S134–S147.

Warner, J., N. Ellman, & D. Boesch. (2018). *The women's leadership gap: Women's leadership by the numbers.* Center for American Progress.

2

TRAUMA-INFORMED PRACTICE AS THE FOUNDATION FOR POSITIVE DISRUPTION

Environments that are trauma-informed are generally healing spaces where the totality of the clients' experience is taken into account. Service providers work with clients in spaces characterized by safety, collaboration, choice, trustworthiness and empowerment in an effort to avoid any re-traumatization. It is true that trauma-informed practice is a guide for service providers to assist in moving the lens beyond the single traumatic event in an effort to understand how the individual has made sense of their world. It is a practice that holds trauma at the center in how an individual or group session, classroom, meeting space and organization is structured and how people move through that structure, at every level. Yet, while this practice is grounded in a good intention ideology, what is missing is a critical analysis and integration of race and culture, not as an afterthought but as a guiding principle of trauma-informed practice. There are several factors that must be taken in to account in order for an environment to truly be a healing space of non-revictimization. First, who and how we define trauma is central to how trauma is understood and operationalized in theory and practice. Second, the social location and the training of the practitioner, leader and educator is a crucial factor in the attempts to create trauma-informed systems of care and avoid re-traumatization. Third, as we will discuss in more detail in a later chapter, the extent to which social work students, educators, practitioners and leaders were, and are still, socialized and educated in a white supremacy framework, lays the foundation for how trauma specific concepts are defined, understood and operationalized. Unless there is an active attempt to deconstruct and positively disrupt normalized ways of knowing and being, that are only grounded in a white ideology, social workers and leaders in the trauma field, may remain oblivious to skewed definitions, exclusionary actions and unintentionally re-traumatize the very clients we aim to help. The actions of social workers become normalized, assumptions are made and unchecked implicit bias can result when there is not an attempt to positively disrupt spaces that are traditionally deemed as trauma-informed. I argue that exclusionary social work practice, particularly in the field of trauma, are the result of social workers not learning how to locate themselves and take time perhaps in supervision or personal therapy, to peel back the layers of socialization, education and training, all of which heavily impact social work practice.

This chapter links the trauma-informed principles of safety, choice, collaboration, trust and empowerment with social work practice and leadership along with a critical awareness of inclusion and diversity. Yet, because the trauma literature and practice are situated in a white normative space, achieving this type of trauma-informed, diverse and inclusive social work practice and leadership requires positive disruption of white normative definitions and spaces. Within this intersection of trauma-informed practice and diversity and inclusion, there is an innate intentionality required from the practitioner and leader which at times can be exhausting because of what is required to hold space for all identities, experiences and traumas. This means challenging the unintentional and exclusionary practices that impact BIPOC that are ingrained in the social work profession, and in particular, in the field of trauma-informed practice. BIPOC is an acronym that stands for Black, Indigenous, people of color that was crafted in 2013 but became more prevalent and popularized on the internet in the aftermath of the killing of George Floyd. Part of challenging exclusionary practices means integrating the mindfulness and presence into your practice that is required to notice when experiences and voices of marginalized communities are missing from the narrative/ Integrating and maintaining the mindfulness and presence into social work practice while subsequently disrupting that narrative continuously and (eventually) habitually is very tiresome. This is even more emotionally taxing if you are a student, leader or practitioner of color. Now more than ever, social workers and leaders in the field are in need of this type of lens as some witness and others experience the racial trauma that permeates this country and has, for the most part, been normalized. Remember, inclusion takes intentional mindfulness to consider anything outside of the familiar and comfortable ways of knowing. Trauma-informed practice is an ideology that is ripe for inclusion and diversity. It is not an intervention or a check list. It is a way of being that fosters physical and emotional safety, choice, collaboration, trust and empowerment at every level of an organization, most importantly at the level of social work practice and leadership.

Locating Myself

From a space of vulnerability, I would like to let you in on my reflective and trauma-informed process as I write. I realize I try to be very cognizant of my research lens and mindful about how I write this part of the story. I am aware of the words I use and the tone I take that will help not only tell this story, but make it accessible to all but uncomfortable for some. I also learned that when writing about race there is an aversion from my white colleagues in the field to look deeply at words such as race, racism, white supremacy and systemic racism and engage in honest and sincere dialogue. Being white is a racial identity too but never talked about and often never thought about. In order to work through this aversion, I locate myself in order for you, the reader, to see my connection to and experience with trauma. This is how my process is trauma-informed. I identify as a Latina and Jewish woman of color from a biracial and multicultural background who is also a single mother of two young girls and a professor who has access to resources, platforms and knowledge. We see in the locating of myself the complexity of identity and the holding of both privileges and oppressions. This is the first step to entering this particular discussion with you. My personal experiences of racism, anti-semitism, sexism and classism are interwoven throughout, as you have read and will continue to do so, yet I feel that if I take on an emotional tone in my writing, or engage in generalizations, some white identified readers may stop reading or at the very least create defensive responses to my words. When I am teaching or training, I tell my students and participants that those shifts in your seat or sudden need to defend or check out is the very material you must work with. It is those moments of felt discomfort that need tending to in order to sincerely locate yourself in the material being taught or presented. I am witnessing my intentionality and mindfulness as I write and finding it sometimes difficult to balance my emotion and my words. I share this with you, the reader, because as social workers our identities intersect with we touch and every space we enter, literally and figuratively. I see my role as the author not to convince you, but rather to create an awareness that leads to action. There may be parts of my story that you disagree with and that is fine. Pay attention to your reactions and your moments of dissonance. Write down the moments you wish to disengage and disengage if you have to. But I ask that after this disengagement, you return attempting to understand and work through those emotions to focus them more productively. I ask that you engage in a willingness to be challenged, without judgment or a "hierarchies of oppression" (Lorde, 1983) debate and commit to being on the journey of learning, growth and change grounded in reflection and inquiry. I also ask that you start by locating yourself in order to listen deeply.

Extreme Lived Experience of COVID 19 and the Resurgence of the Black Lives Matter Movement

In order to situate where I am physically, spiritually and mentally, I am writing this project during the COVID-19 pandemic, and the concurrent protests surrounding the Black Lives Matter movement and calls to defund oppressive government institutions. The COVID-19 experience influences behavior and triggers responses just like any other traumatic event would, just with more breadth and intensity. For Black, Indigenous, communities of color there is a complexity to this trauma because of the lived experience of interpersonal and systemic racism. What this extreme, pandemic experience allows us is an opportunity to see very clearly how trauma-informed work is relevant and necessary. The impact of COVID-19 may force social workers to think deeper concerning issues of race and social justice, and issues of diversity, equity and inclusion especially as it applies to direct service employees and the communities and people they serve. Compounding this impact and trauma are questions surrounding the revitalization and increased interest and support behind the Black Lives Matter movement. I grapple with the question of why now? Why do white people now care about the murders of Black people? Without a pandemic happening would this be the case? Does the privilege of sheltering in place give us the unique opportunity to watch and learn because society is less busy? This pandemic does offer a unique opportunity as a researcher to be able to critically assess how the impact and response is differential across lines of culture, class and race. Responses and reactions to COVID-19 serve as a demonstration for the need to create and facilitate trauma-informed practice from the lens of inclusion and diversity. I am seeing trauma in so many spaces and with that, the complexity of this trauma. Specifically, how trauma touches people in different ways, all of which deserves attention. I am reminded of my research on both trauma-informed practice and inclusion. I see so clearly the opportunity to positively disrupt spaces that do not give voice to the experiences of groups who have been scapegoated, the undocumented people, the working class people who cannot afford to "shelter-in-place" and the families who depend on the stability, structure and food delivered by school systems across the country. I also see how one can work from a traditional trauma-informed lens and still exclude those who are most vulnerable.

I am reminded of the intentional mindfulness needed in order to operate from the place of trauma-informed inclusion and diversity in order to honor the diverse outlooks and experiences that people have in this real-life example. Some of the questions I am reflecting on are how are we entering this experience? Are we examining our own personal positionalities and experiences, along with critically examining the pandemic's disparate impact on families and local communities? As a single, working mom with two school age kids my needs are pulled in different directions but my lens is not myopic and so I strive to be in a space of both gratitude and collective vulnerability. I strive to wake up in a space of gratitude every day and with the goal of disrupting at least one space that is silent to the experiences of others who are vulnerable. I am helping my clients, students, friends and colleagues see the intersection of trauma, diversity and inclusion because we are living it. For many, this pandemic has disrupted and challenged the view of the world. For some, it is a reminder of the daily challenges of living in fear and the everyday occurrences of traumatic experiences shaped by social structures. I have had social workers and leaders in organizations ask how to incorporate diversity and inclusion into this space. My response is widening the lens and adopting a trauma-informed ideology of inclusion that positively disrupts spaces that exclude the most vulnerable.

Many carry scars of marginalization and discrimination based on race, gender, class and culture. This is not true for my personal community of white friends, including my mom, who do not live with such everyday distress. Living with trauma of survival is normalized for Black, Indigenous, communities of color and the impact is felt on many levels. For many white folks, this pandemic engages with fear and uncertainty in a way that is so new and so frightening and this anxiety of survival manifests in different ways. I look at the behavior of the stockpiling of toilet paper, an item whose availability and use are in no way changed by the pandemic or its symptoms. Can the emotional toil of this pandemic be a starting point for white individuals and communities to see a glimpse of how racism is experienced by Black, Indigenous and people of color every day?

Trauma is very much connected to the individual who experiences a sense of emotional risk or constant stress or inability to navigate the world calmly. The psychological experience of the traumatized individual becomes paramount, yet not all clients and not all post-trauma reactions are treated with the same kid gloves. We are likely to see a disparity in the treatment of clients if the practitioner does not engage in the initial practice of locating oneself. Here is where we started this chapter. How are traumas defined and classified? What traumas do social workers hold as legitimate and as paramount? How do ways of knowing impact the practice? As practitioners in positions of power, have we learned to unpack and check implicit bias at the beginning of our work with clients and throughout the process? In the COVID-19 case, as in all-natural disasters, there is a consensually agreed upon criteria. The classification of this event is traumatic. When trauma of this nature impacts the dominant culture, the response is different. Post-trauma reactions are "understood," and allowances are given. Outside of the state of emergency and exception, the traumas of systemic racism do not have an agreed upon criteria and are not always recognized as traumas. In addition, the post-traumatic reactions such as those seen in the Black Lives Matter movement including the resurgence of the movement and protests, are questioned, judged, and not seen or understood through the lens of post-trauma reactions to historical and systemic trauma.

Trauma-Informed Practice from a Diversity and Inclusion Lens

Trauma-Informed Spaces

Focus on trauma-informed practice principles has recently begun to emerge in schools of social, healthcare facilities, mental health agencies and other organizations. This is very positive as clients are more likely to be viewed through a person-in-environment and holistic lens. In general, this approach encourages all members of an organization to have a comprehensive understanding of the effects and complexity of trauma, its potential behavioral manifestations, and principles for addressing the needs of traumatized clients. To become trauma-informed, a system of care must demonstrate understanding and recognition of trauma as both interpersonal *and* sociopolitical and foster physical and emotional safety, trustworthiness, choice, collaboration and empowerment at all levels of service delivery (Fallot & Harris 2009). Yet, most traditional models of trauma-informed practice operate within the existing white normative culture. Instead of an explicit overarching lens of inclusion and diversity, inclusion and diversity become a bullet point and an achievable goal labeled as "culturally responsive practice." This is similar to the discussion we had in the previous chapter on cultural competency, and this issue of white normative framing exists in many different disciplines. Working within systems that are deemed as trauma-informed does not necessarily mean they are racially or culturally sensitive, inclusive or diverse spaces. Trauma-informed does not mean that the principles of trauma-informed care (safety, trustworthiness, choice, collaboration and empowerment) are inclusive of the realities of marginalized communities, particularly communities of color. For example, the principle of safety shows up very differently depending on one's positionality. For Black, Indigenous, people of color, physical, spiritual and emotional safety cannot be assumed. The impact of working in predominately white spaces alone, on top of daily microaggressions that inevitably show up in the workplace, often result in an uneasiness of being and potentially threaten the physical, spiritual and emotional safety of Black, Indigenous, people of color. Unless educators, researchers and leaders in the social work field make an explicit commitment to positively disrupt the traditional trauma-informed discourse to include the experience of being a person of color in a predominately white space, white normative culture prevails and implicit bias and microaggressions become a part of the classroom and the organizational culture. Furthermore, there will inevitably be a trickledown effect to social workers' practice with clients and communities of color. As we discussed, creating diverse and inclusive spaces requires an organizational commitment that begins with educators, researchers and leadership, peeling back the layers to have brave and uncomfortable conversations on a consistent basis about the realities of systemic racism and the fields' complicity in upholding white supremacy. Simply administering a training is not enough. In my research and consulting practice, I have not come across training and consulting models other than my own that suggest positive disruption of the trauma-informed space. Organizations typically are either driven towards a trauma-informed mission, or diversity, equity and inclusion. These ways of practice are treated as mutually exclusive.

Furthermore, I have found in my consulting and research that conceptualizations of trauma are rigid and narrow. Many who go into the field of trauma have been trained to see trauma in a monolithic way. Even those who work with the trauma from natural disasters that differentially impact communities of color rarely include a racial lens or interrogate the trauma of the normalization of whiteness. Thus, social workers in the field of trauma, educators and researchers often fail to recognize structural trauma such as racism, and silo their trauma work to only the interpersonal. Research in this field has traditionally omitted analysis of structural racism and whiteness as part of the complete trauma narrative. In responding to the sociopolitical complexity of trauma: An Integration of Theory and Practice (Quiros & Berger, 2013) my colleague, Dr. Roni Berger, and I offer a definition that broadens the scope of trauma-informed practice by including the sociopolitical complexity of trauma. This sociopolitical complexity includes awareness of the intersectionality of race, class and gender, and underscores that consideration of these intersections are essential for the creation of organizations that are truly trauma-informed. What distinguishes this current project is its multifaceted approach to trauma-informed practice, which aims to capture the full trauma narrative by intersecting practice and issues around inclusion, diversity and positive disruption.

It is my belief that an agency that is trauma-informed must also *explicitly* adopt a lens of diversity and inclusion if it is aligned with a mission of social justice. It is only through this explicit, intentional lens that structural and environmental conditions are considered when assessing trauma. Failure to effectively adopt this specific kind of trauma-informed care as an integral aspect of social work practice and agency culture may potentially put social work and human service programs out of sync with an organizational commitment to social justice. Trauma is "a reaction to a kind of wound. It is a reaction to profoundly injurious events and situations in the real world and, indeed, to a world in which people are routinely wounded" (Burstow, 2003) and thus, traumatizing socio-political circumstances must be part of the understanding and addressing of people's psychosocial problems.

Intentional Disruption Through My Scholarship

I have done quite a bit of research, practice and writing on trauma-informed practice and disrupting this space, yet the paper I am most proud of is called Disrupting the Single Story: Challenging Dominate Trauma Narratives through a Critical Race Lens (Quiros, Varghese, & Vanidestine, 2020. This was a collaborative effort of labor and love. I wrote this article with two of my colleagues, and friends, who live and breathe through a lens of social justice. A cisgender woman of South Asian descent, Dr. Rani Varghese, and a cisgender white male from Maine, Dr. Todd Vanidestine. In this article we used a few tenets of critical race theory to disrupt the trauma narrative and make connections between both fields. Specifically, we discussed the ordinariness of racism, differential racialization and counter storytelling narratives. Critical Race Theory, as a theoretical framework, provided us with a counternarrative voice to positively disrupt the traditional trauma space. This article explicitly addresses a gap in the trauma literature that does not take up racial oppression as a form of "trauma" and ultimately disrupts the trauma narrative by centering race, racism and whiteness. The first time through the article was rejected. However, in the editor comments we noticed that the feedback was very subjective, most likely based on the editor's positionality. As professors we lived under an implicit rule of accepting the comments of the reviewer in the peer review process. Yet, as the first author, I took on the task of questioning the editor, and coming from a place of curiosity. I asked specific questions related to the comments we received. Such as:

ME: *The reviewers' comments are starkly different. While one reviewer (Reviewer #2) describes our manuscript as "well written and organized" and sees it making a contribution to the field of traumatology, the other reviewer (Reviewer #1) describes it as full of "grammatical errors [and] incomplete sentences" and based in "sweeping generalizations" limiting its "utility and contribution." What felt disarming to us was how Reviewer # 1, not only disputed the experiences we wrote about as "trauma," but the Reviewer also seemed unable to hold trauma, race and racism at the same time. While we are open to critiques (i.e. "paper written for social work journal," "lack of precision in language," or "rely on single sources too often") and revising our work, I would be remiss not to express our disappointment.*

EDITOR: *Your work is important, but please note this is a highly competitive journal and the editorial board reviewers are some of the best in the world. The reviewer who rejected your paper has over 100 publications and is one of the foremost trauma scholars in the world, so I trust their judgment.*

I also emphasized the fact that this "disruption" was critical at a time when inclusion and diversity were trending. In addition, we were filling a gap in the trauma literature by interrogating and disrupting whiteness. We were eventually offered to revise and resubmit the paper. My colleagues and I made some technical edits, added some context and the paper was accepted with the initial discussion and content intact.

After resubmitting the paper for publication, I returned to the initial feedback and realized there was a lot to unpack. For one, I was struck by the Editors defense of Reviewer 1's credentials, when we were attempting to disrupt the status quo. Second, Reviewer 1's micro aggressions directed towards our grammatical errors rather than the content of our paper. Reviewer 1s' brash response may speak more to the ways that their own way of being was disrupted rather than whether or not the argument in the paper added new scholarship to the field. I also realize that the work my colleagues and I were presenting may have undermined the sweeping generalizations that Reviewer 1 himself has made in the field. Finally, the fact that the Editor is trusting the judgment of the Reviewer, but ultimately siding against them in deciding to publish the paper speaks volumes and potentially validates the aforementioned deconstruction.

Locating Yourself

In the beginning of this chapter I used the real life and extreme example of COVID-19 and the resurgence of the Black Lives Matter movement to illustrate the need to create and facilitate trauma-informed practice from the lens of inclusion and diversity. I wrote about the complexity of trauma as it relates to class and race, and the need to first locate ourselves to understand our positionality in order to inform how we are entering any discussion. This begins as an internal dialogue and then extends outward to others. Within this transmission of sharing one's social location, pay careful attention to the parts that feel uncomfortable; the narratives that do not flow as easily and the ways you move in and out of internal and external dialogue. This is where mindfulness intersects with vulnerability. Becoming mindful of and about our triggers and then vulnerable enough to share in an effort to engage in dialogue. As hooks (1994) taught us:

> To engage in dialogue is one of the simplest ways we can begin as [people], teachers, scholars and critical thinkers to cross boundaries, the barriers that may or may not be erected by race, gender, class, professional standing and a host of other differences. (p. 130).

Truly inclusive trauma-informed organizations and classrooms begin with leaders and educators who are able to locate themselves and view the system through a lens of inclusion and diversity with the understanding that trauma includes a sociopolitical complexity, and a need to positively disrupt to create transformational change.

Reflection and Discussion Questions

When people are exposed to traumatic experiences who are not usually exposed to trauma of this sort, as in the COVID-19 pandemic, specifically when it is about survival, what opportunities for compassion, connection and communication does this open? I wonder in all of this, are social workers locating themselves, thinking about each other and engaging in dialogue about the intersections of trauma and race? Are we, as educators and leaders in the field, explicitly naming structural racism as a trauma that has historically impacted communities of color as we see the research on health disparities revealed again? Are people taking care of their own while also considering how others are struggling with this? And on a meta level, in a society where vulnerability is not seen as a strength, how do we train our leaders to lead through a trauma-informed lens of vulnerability and inclusion?

On many different levels, the country, collectively and individually, is currently in a state of complex trauma and there is an opportunity here to shift, collectively and individually, to a heart space of inclusion. In times of crisis such as this, what help do leaders need to lead, "see" and respond to the multitude of issues created and exacerbated by the current state of crisis? Most importantly, how do we incorporate these questions, this way of collective being, into our permanent national discourse?

Trauma-informed leadership through a diversity and inclusion lens honors all the complexity of trauma with the caveat of vulnerability and a desire for positive disruption. Acknowledgement and acceptance of the fact that this may cost you some of your privileges is a requirement. For some leaders these privileges are self-imposed such as the privilege of being seen as all-knowing and invincible and for others the privileges are more tangible. The first step in this work is to identify what this is for you? What are you willing to sacrifice for inclusion? Are you able to craft a lens that engages your heart and your head and honors complexity and vulnerability?

This chapter is chock-full with opportunities for reflection and discussion. The above questions are made for a journal entry, a coaching exercise, a small group exercise or a larger forum. Take some time to write down the above reflection questions in the above two paragraphs and answer them to the best of your ability. While you are answering the questions, pay close attention to how you feel when you answer the questions. Where are you stumbling? What feels hard to write down or say out loud? What feels easy to answer or say out loud? Try to write from a place of compassion for yourself without judgment.

References

Burstow, B. (2003). Toward a radical understanding of trauma and trauma work. *Violence against Women*, 9 (11), 1293–1317.

Fallot, R. D., & Harris, M. (2009). *Creating cultures of trauma-informed care (CCTIC): A self-assessment and planning protocol. Washington, DC, USA: Community Connections.*

hooks, b. (1994). *Teaching to transgress.* New York, NY: Routledge.

Lorde, A. (1983). There is no hierarchy of oppression. *Bulletin: Homophobia and Education*, 14, 9.

Quiros, L., & Berger, R. (2013). Responding to the sociopolitical complexity of trauma: An integration of theory and practice. *Journal of Loss and Trauma: International Perspectives on Stress & Coping*, 20(2), 149–159.

Quiros, L., Varghese, R., & Vanidestine, T. (2020). Disrupting the single story: Challenging dominant trauma narratives through a critical race lens. *Traumatology*, 26(2), 160–168.

3

LEADERSHIP IN SOCIAL WORK

Locating Myself

As I sit here thinking, I am struggling with how to define leadership from an objective standpoint. I am not certain that this is possible because so much of occupying a leadership space is grounded in early life lessons and experiences. I could go immediately to the literature but before I do that, I need to understand my personal connection to leadership and so, I call on the practice principle of locating myself first.

I think about the times in my life when I was met knowingly or unknowingly with a leadership role. Reflecting on my own experience to try to locate how I was socialized into understanding leadership; my first memory is on the soccer field. From the ages of ten to nineteen, I was a goal keeper. I played on many teams from my town's recreational league, to travel teams, to my high school team and had a short stint as a goal keeper for a Division 3 College. I am a sum total of my experiences and so it would make sense that when thinking about how to enter the space of leadership for this project, I would draw upon my memories on the soccer field, as part of a team occupying the role of a goal keeper. Team sports, in general, played a significant role in my life and taught me the skills of relationship building, determination, inclusion, aggression, perseverance, success and defeat. My dedicated participation on sports teams is responsible for my natural skills of collaboration, trust and my ideology and practice of teamwork. Yet, the role of a goal keeper is one that speaks to the juxtaposition of individuality within the context of a team because it is an isolating and lonely role and also carries the weight of leadership. Focus, concentration and the ability to accept your mistakes and handle pressure are hallmarks of the position. It is the person that can see the landscape of the field, can run the game by assisting players with positioning by communicating, and ultimately puts themselves in the line of fire to defend the net. There are back and forth of moments of pure solitude and silence followed immediately by a one-on-one interaction with a sudden strike of a ball. Ultimately, the goal keeper is vulnerable to attack as the last line of defense. It is an intensely psychological position that requires mental and physical strength as well as a great deal of humility. The dominant narrative after any game is always about who scored the most goals, not who defended the most shots. In this reflection I see clearly how my socialization to a leadership role involved a sense of humility, vulnerability and an organic use of self that was grounded in relationship building and collaboration, where everyone has something different to contribute and the metaphorical "win" is a win for all. Diversity and inclusion are crucial in creating a balanced team, with different identities, strengths and weaknesses. This balance is only possible through tenets of diversity and inclusion, and without said principles the team is left unbalanced and susceptible. Winning the game becomes more difficult. As the person at the end of the field, watching all the pieces of this puzzle come together is both magical and beautiful, even when it does not result in a win.

Once I have located myself, I turn to the literature on leadership, which includes the role of the social work supervisor as a leader in establishing a culture within their team. The leadership narrative and literature start from a place where white culture is the norm

2. Are we explicitly asking this question?
3. And if we aren't then why not?

Now introducing how gender may further alienate and force negotiation of identity, I include women of color in this discussion as I have sat in executive meetings when disparities in gender are addressed. Yet, the lens of intersectionality is not open. Gender disparities in the workplace are certainly real; coupled with being a Black woman in white organizational culture is an experience in and of itself. In my experience, the stories of what it is like to be Black and Brown and female in white spaces gets debated, blocked with defensives, gets rushed to fix, or excludes the story tellers. When these stories are laid bare from a place of rawness, rarely are the stories allowed to marinate and settle from a point of reflection instead of from a place of defensiveness, denial of experience and conflation. This is also a place where we see the hierarchy of oppression debate (Lorde, 1983) emerge among white woman, who yearn for an equal seat at the oppression table. Focusing on the marginalization and oppression of Black and Brown women does not cancel out the marginalization of white women, but this becomes the backlash of centering the experiences of Black women. When centering a discussion around any persons' identity or experiences, we should strive to mindfully and compassionately understand a persons' traumatic experiences and consider our part in perpetuating or acting indifferently toward these experiences, especially when we ourselves have been oppressed. Hierarchy of oppression debates are an act of oppression and often arise from deeper senses of guilt and an aversion to hold yourself accountable. As Lorde (1983) stated, "there is no hierarchy of oppression" if the goal is liberation for all.

When truth telling narratives surrounding issues of diversity and inclusion are not able to be censored or silenced, leadership and administration will accept and promote the need to conduct diversity and inclusion work. Truth-telling narratives unveil the realties and lived experiences of Black, Indigenous and people of color. Once the veil is lifted it is harder to deny the experiences of exclusion and of systemic racism. However, more often than not, these attempts at diversity are strictly performative. This is frequently done by hiring leaders of color for quantitative publicity. In my work as a consultant and as a professor, I hear things like "diversify the board," "increase the hiring of Black and Brown partners," "bring in more diversity." This focus on bodies only provides an institution of whiteness with color. "Diversity becomes about *changing perceptions of whiteness rather than changing the whiteness of the organization*," (Ahmed, 2012). While perceptions can be changed by said quantitative measures and performatives, it takes a change of culture through our work to change whiteness. In certain organizations, the diversity of workforce and leadership may serve as a means to disguise and deflect entirely, intentionally or unintentionally, an examination of whiteness and racism in an organization's culture, policy and legacy. Furthermore, if Brown and Black bodies do occupy leadership spaces in an organization where diversity, equity and inclusion are less valued by the organization, their bodies alone become the diversity and the work becomes less valued (Ahmed, 2012). If leadership remains grounded in white ideology these diverse bodies may only survive by adopting and centering whiteness. If we get used to whiteness (it can be a survival strategy to learn not to see it, to learn not to see how you are not reflected back by what is around), it does not mean whiteness does not still affect us (Ahmed, 2012).

Positive Disruption

In some ways, this required positive disruption of dominant narratives as the norm, is working toward the impossibility of changing mindsets to allow for a desire to understand one another and share space. There are countless examples of the precarity involved with positive disruption especially for untenured faculty, adjunct faculty, social workers on the front line and students. Because there are no best practices for this work, some of these individuals and groups might choose docility in the institution in order to survive, persevere and/or "choose your battle." A concrete example comes to mind; I was leading and facilitating a training for adjunct faculty and supervisors, and a woman of color was lamenting over her fear of bringing up the issue of structural racism in her class. Made up of primarily white social work students, she was worried that addressing issues leadership arena? The freedom to just speak is not a reality. Can I even envision a type of leadership that is inclusive of my identities and also acknowledging of the triple consciousness experienced by women of color in this role? Welang (2018) expands DuBois (1903) concept of Double Consciousness by drawing attention to the three lenses that Black women view themselves through, "*America* (represented by the hegemony of white patriarch), *Blackness* (A radical space that prioritize the interests of the Black man), *womanhood* (a hierarchical gendered identity with white women at the top and Black women at the bottom)" (Welang, 2018). This theory gives voice to my experience as a Latina woman in leadership and the parameters of identity that I was constantly confronting alongside of how I was consistently socially constructed. It felt like a sociological constraint, not very different from the women whom I worked with in the treatment center. Not being seen for who I am, in my totality and being asked to fit into a space of leadership that is both defined by and made for by white men and white women. Who am I in this space and how do I operate from a place of wholeness? Can they see me beyond just my body and the social constructions of race, gender and culture? If I do not locate myself first while acknowledging the limitations of traditional theoretical frameworks and practice models, I am never going to be able to come to a liberated and true self. In this instance, although the white female trainer and I may share a similar identity in a predominantly male-centered field, I have another identity that I struggle to incorporate and that is my identity as a biracial Latina. I am part of the minority and so what this training was telling me was somehow authenticity was synonymous with a white existence because that was the dominant discourse. Whiteness is again valued, maintained and normalized. The dominate discourse has the power to narrate the story of what it means to be authentic and, in this instance, the power to define and teach "authentic leadership." Again, here in lies the juxtaposition, docility or disruption, both equally precarious and both choices have implications for self-identity and self-identification.

I was not the only woman of color in the room and I remember scanning the audience, looking for any nonverbal cues but the audience sat in attention, no one was even on the verge of raising their hands. My internal dialogue continued, how come the assigned leaders of this social work academy, an academy grounded in a mission of social justice, do not speak to the intersectionality of gender and race? Why does social work, a field which prides itself on its holistic person-in-environment approach to problem solving, not question the tenets of authentic leadership? I stayed quiet during the training because I did not feel safe or comfortable challenging the hegemony of white leadership alone. This feeling of lack of safety was a feeling of precarity. That if I spoke up and questioned the academy, my job and future leadership positions within the academy would be at stake. I did approach the organizer of the event at the end of the training and asked if there was a session during this leadership retreat devoted to leaders of color within the academy. The answer was "*no, but how great for you to organize that.*" This is a common response. The academy was not doing this work, so essentially, I was being asked to develop and "do" the diversity and inclusion work in a space where that work and my body was not seen or valued. There was not a financial or emotional investment in the academy trying to understand the lived experiences of leaders of color or the white normative ideology that was inherently exclusive. Instead, they wanted the leaders of color to do the work and educate them using us and our experiences as the learning tool. What kind of institutional support and backing is there when leaders of color have to ignite and drive diversity and inclusion work themselves? The necessity to be the sole igniter and driver of diversity and inclusion projects works to undermine and jeopardize its full realization as this means the institution and its resources will merely watch you try to succeed in bringing a project to life, rather than supporting your effort to succeed. Failed or unsuccessful projects then serve as evidence for lack of necessity or interest in the organization in diversity and inclusion participation. I imagined that in this case, the diversity work would be about the experiences of leaders of color rather than reflecting on the normalization of the institutionalization of whiteness. I ended up developing a training with the hopes of raising awareness and making room for a different voice, without any expectations of anything more than that.

COVID-19 and Leadership

Immediately prior to the COVID-19 pandemic, I had a sense that some leaders were beginning to personally grapple with whiteness and make room for the sincere integration of diversity, equity and inclusion in leadership, beyond the office of Human Resources. *White Fragility* by Robin DiAngelo became a must read for many organizations and some leadership teams were even openly talking about whiteness, white privilege and white fragility as they slowly moved toward action of institutionalizing missions of diversity, equity and inclusion. I attribute this to a trend, a backlash against the political climate, as well as a genuine shift from the head space to the heart space of this work. And then came COVID-19.

Response to COVID-19 and The Murder of George Floyd

I noticed in my consulting and in my work at the University that once the pandemic hit, diversity, equity and inclusion became siloed, it was not a felt need and so the "work" was no longer a priority. Creating inclusive, diverse and equitable spaces was not given the same worth or value as fundraising or remote learning for example. This begged the question of, *what do leaders place value on, especially when things get choppy?* If diversity, equity and inclusion work were dedicated to a one-off training or delegated to a committee or task force of diverse constituents and was not something leaders were pushing within a heart space, it fell to the wayside. In one organization I work with the diversity, equity and inclusion committee was "put on a hold," until the organization "returned to normal." The irony is that this real life and extreme event is the perfect place to engage in trauma-informed leadership from a diversity and inclusion lens. What a better time for white folks to engage in a deeper sense of compassion for the lived and everyday experiences of Black, Indigenous and people of color. What a better time to begin to understand the impact of being "locked up." What a better time to grapple with the contradiction of essential and expendable employees. What a better time to positively disrupt conversations about racial health disparities with dialogues about the history and impact of structural racism. What a better time to see the intersections of racism and ageism.

And then George Floyd was murdered by a Minnesota police officer. Once the outrage, pain and resulting protests hit the country, I started receiving an onslaught of emails from organizations asking for help. Organizations, ranging in size from large non-profits to smaller for-profit business startups, reached out for help with messaging, help with holding healing circles, help with resources and help with processing all of the violence, trauma, pain and shame. I had organizations whose contracts had recently expired and initially had no interest in renewal, return to renew contracts to develop more programming and coaching. Some of these organizations had initially, a year or a few months ago, felt like they did not need help in the area of diversity, equity and inclusion but now were anxious and unhinged, desperate to connect and ready to act. The felt immediacy and anxiety was visceral in the phone calls and in the emails I received. For white executives there was real fear in not knowing what to do with their own feelings and what to say to staff and, even more, how to hold space to listen to the pain of racial trauma and exclusion among Black, Indigenous and people of color.

The organizations who did not jump ship at the onset of COVID-19, the larger non-profits, had a much easier time transitioning into addressing the pain and moving into action. Messages were immediately sent out; a forum was created to bring staff together and healing circles were put into place. I coached executives and members of the executive teams on language and facilitated the forum. But I mostly remained in the background as a sounding board and for support, helping leaders in the organization who were already deeply involved with social justice work.

On the flip side there were the organizations, for-profit businesses and start-ups, primarily, run by white CEOs with a predominately white leadership team. One of the organizations had to let me go at the onset of COVID-19 because they were financially hit hard and had to furlough about 96% of their staff. The organization is a music driven exercise business, whose sincere work in the diversity, equity and inclusion space started in 2018. I was referred to them by a colleague and the initial work centered on responding to an email from a client of color who felt that the owners were engaging in cultural appropriation because they were centering hip hop as the music to exercise to, yet they were primarily a white lead organization. The owner herself is multicultural but no one on their leadership team was Black identified. There was the sentiment among some clients that only Black led organizations can center hip hop as their music. The CEO was challenged by not only how to respond to the client's email but how to open up the exercise space to a more diverse clientele even though this particular form of exercise in New York City is primarily a white space. The unpacking and responding of that email lead us down a road of sincere inclusion work. I held sessions with their entire staff on a range of issues and skills, from community building, whiteness, implicit bias and instruction from the lens of diversity and inclusion, to even working closely with marketing to diversify images that not only highlighted instructors of color, but also diverse body images. After beginning my work with this organization on every level, leadership began to establish relationships with communities of color where the hope was that they could bring this form of practice into the school system, and I was responsible for helping to promote employees of color to more senior positions. In my years working for them I had developed a close relationship with their Head of People who is a white woman. We worked closely on her own journey of understanding and owning her white privilege and unearned white advantages. We traveled to their other studios in Los Angeles and worked with the team there, providing similar trainings and centering sessions around a lens of inclusion and diversity. I facilitated dialogues and workshops that asked staff to locate themselves and make connections between their exercise practice and diversity, equity and inclusion. Many had never had the opportunity to dialogue about how their backgrounds and familial messages show up in the way they lead their class, which clients they unconsciously give more attention to, or how the language they use in the class could be exclusionary. We built community together as the CEOs trusted me to work closely with their teams and all members of the organization.

When the protests started, social media became the platform of expression. I noticed that it specifically became a space of accountability. People from all identities were holding others and organizations accountable and looking, very closely, at what organizations, especially white lead organizations, were messaging. There was significant pressure to turn out a message fast, post a statement and an action attached to that statement. I received a call from this organization asking for help with the messaging. We created a statement from the owner, sharing how this work started with a crisis but evolved into an intentional and mindful journey into diversity, equity and inclusion. I coached them to put out a call to action for other exercise spaces to do the same. This was an organization that was hit hard financially and offered the funds they received from the small business loan to pay me. Rather than accept this, I asked that they use the funds to bring back Black, Indigenous, employees of color and as long as this condition was met, I would work pro bono and support the organization in their diversity, equity and inclusion efforts with the Black staff they hired back. They did just that and we worked together to facilitate a Town Hall.

Around the same time, I received a call from three other for-profit organizations. All start-ups but none of them were impacted financially by COVID-19. Except for a one-off implicit bias training, these organizations had never done any sustained work in diversity, equity or inclusion. My point of contact was again the Head of People, also known as Human Resources, followed by calls with the CEOs. For many of these organizations, the work of diversity and inclusion lives in the space of Human Resources, yet many who hold this position are ill equipped to engage with this work, especially the white women who dominate leadership roles in this field. While HR or "People" or "People Ops" works has been expanded to be more strategic over the last ten years, diversity, equity and inclusion has only recently become a piece of the strategy, and HR is ill-equipped for it. HR/People leaders are overwhelmingly white cisgender women. This in and of itself sets the stage for a lack of understanding of how one fits into systems of oppression that are present in and out of the workplace. White and cisgender women in these leadership roles often do not spend time in their private or professional lives working through this. The result is that the majority of these women do not know how to have one-on-one conversations with employees on the subject of race nor build equitable or inclusive companies. Here we see a role that social workers can play in coaching or upskilling HR/People leaders in any organization.

Prior to agreeing to begin the work with these organizations and with these leaders, we reached an agreement that these trainings and priority on diversity, equity and inclusion would be sustained in the long term. Two organizations jumped right in. We quickly put together a forum, organized dialogues for staff in different departments, and messaged to employees that the organization had committed to this work for the long haul. I was struck by one organization in particular, whose CEOs presented themselves as particularly nervous. This organization was run by a white man and a white woman and they described themselves as "Co-CEOS." I sat on a call with them one Saturday evening to talk about my work and what the forum that they requested would look like. The call evolved into me convincing them of not so much why this work was important, but that it was organic in nature and they had to trust the process. They were anxious to "get it right" and driven by a sense of urgency to respond but unable to say how they want to respond. The woman CEO shared her usual practice with me, which was driven by perfectionism, planning, researching and reviewing any material before it was shared with others, sent out and before any action was taken. When public outrage ensued following the murders of Ahmaud Arbery, Breonna Taylor and George Floyd, she was paralyzed with how to respond and what actions to put in place. She operated from a lens of right and wrong, meaning she did not know the right thing to do, and was afraid of doing the wrong thing. We sat on the call for some time and I explained that the work of social justice is imperfect, messy, unpredictable and uncomfortable and that right now they do not have a right to comfort. I explained the work involves taking risks, honoring curiosity, being vulnerable and ultimately speaking from your heart. She was caught in the traditional leadership framework, which led to her being unable to respond sincerely to racism. I imagine and have witnessed that most white CEOs feel the same way. The response to this moment is only felt as sincere through tone and language, not by providing the research to support your statement. They both expressed concern that the forum would become a session of "poking holes in the organization" or that folks would just sit in silence. There was a felt fear of open conflict. I spent time explaining to them that when or if employees do share what has not worked for them, we listen and if we are met with silence, we honor curiosity and ask why we are met with silence. I ended up holding two forums for this organization, the first one was tricky in the sense that employees were not used to this open space to share. Many showed up anxious, uneasiness, uncomfortable and some were hurt by past experiences of racism. The group yearned for more than the allotted one hour that we planned for. The second session was met with a more grounded discussion on hopes and challenges for where employees see the opportunities for diversity and inclusion work and where the organizational structure can expand to be more inclusive and equitable. After each of my facilitated forums, the CEOs and Head of People continued the conversation with those who wanted to stay and dialogue. In total they devoted 6 hours to discussions on race, racism, whiteness and organizational culture. My work with the organization has transitioned into individual coaching for the leadership team and more intimate group work with individual departments.

Social work is a multifaceted profession that offers an array of opportunities in and outside of the social work field. It is here that we revisit the intentional use of self that is critical to helping to change organizational culture. Even in the moments of working outside of the profession, I identify as a social worker and dig into my tool box of years of experience in the field, my personal growth and formal education to positively disrupt spaces that are exclusive. I saw my trauma-informed clinical skills, grounded in a lens of inclusion and diversity, emerge during these moments when I was openly working in collaboration with the leaders. I leaned into skills of group work facilitation, that is, sitting with silence, active listening, using the group to guide the session and modeling transparency and accountability in my approach to critical conversations about race and systemic racism. My use of self was critically important and with each engagement I began by locating myself, quietly and intentionally. I shared with these organizations that my approach is unique because of the intersections of my lenses; trauma and social justice. Approaching and treating complex trauma must be grounded in a social justice approach. I talk explicitly about the pain, inclusion and hope from every angle and hold space for all that pain and all of the possibility. I am very direct in the dialogues with staff in explaining and sharing how I am holding hope and possibility and fear and dread all in this moment, all at the same time. I have to stay hopeful that this moment becomes a movement and also am very aware that as a country and as a people, we have no evidence that this change will come. I am a social worker who believes in change and I also know the impact of complex trauma and how it alters the mind, body and spirit.

I accepted the engagements and opportunities that arose in the wake of the widespread resurgence of the Black Lives Matter movement with the understanding that my work with any organization must be sustained when the fires die. That the work had to be reflective and action oriented. What kept me up at night, for several nights, was the fear that the sincerity of this work would be lost after things "settled". The momentum would die and we would witness a return to "normalcy." A normalcy that is synonymous with white supremacy. I do not have an answer to that yet, but I do know that as a social worker, I am working to train white leaders to connect with their anxieties in this moment, share their fears and offer themselves in vulnerable ways to their staff. My work with Black, Indigenous leaders of color involves finding healing and ways to mobilize anger and frustration into action. The thought that lingers in my mind even while doing this work and holding space for white clients is, it took so long. As discussed, my identity and lived experience as a Latina and Jewish woman of color who herself has experienced racial trauma is never separated from my work. What helps me channel my rage is my higher order purpose of social justice, which cannot be achieved through a place of self-righteousness, and a "talking at." There is a possibility for negative disruption when the dialogue turns into a debate, when divisions within communities of color are centered instead of unity, or when people were on the right path and went wrong somewhere along the way. We do not know where this moment will lead us, or if this moment will turn into a movement. But the possibility of it catalyzing into tangible systemic change and action must be enough to mobilize people and leaders.

It is important to emphasize and endorse the movement's possibility and gradual progress, rather than dwell on the uncertainty as that alone is enough to demobilize large swaths of people. It has taken so long for white leaders to talk about the impact of systemic racism on their leadership, on their organizations and the people they work with and for. I wonder if leaders will continue to build the racial stamina to do the internal work, which means locating themselves, unpacking why it took so long and engaging in actionable steps to address systemic racism that lives in every organizational culture.

All at the same time, I witness the conversations that have surfaced with my white colleagues at the university. An onslaught of resources were shared over email, sometimes without context, yet we still have not sat with one another and dialogued about the realities of faculty and students of color and, despite being a school of social work grounded in a mission of social justice, the complicity in upholding the status quo. Late one night I drafted this note to the community of faculty and administration but never ended up sending it. The precarity felt too real in this moment and I was physically, spiritually and emotionally drained.

Dear Social Work Community,

In this moment I want to encourage you to connect with the core social justice mission of social work. Take some time to reflect on your purpose for pursuing a degree in social work, a career teaching social work and leading in a school of social work.

Can we take more risks as a community to be braver, kinder and educate ourselves in areas related to race and our students and colleagues of color? Can we take more risks to not sit in silence when we hear and see inequity show up in our community?

In times like these, the hardest and most critical part of social work and social justice work is the internal reflection and becoming aware of how we may have been benefiting and contributing to systemic oppression. The next step involves action including creating a community where we can hold each other accountable to uphold the social justice mission of social work through our interactions with one another, our teaching, service and scholarship.

This moment is an opportunity to see very clearly the connections between practice and policy and the trauma of racism. My hope is that we come together as a community and work to help dismantle systemic oppression in our own school, the larger university and the communities we serve.

Finally, I have also been holding space for social work supervisors during this time. Social work supervisors are leaders in organizations. Again, I witness the difficulty with white supervisors not feeling comfortable talking about racism, naming and identifying systemic racism and naming whiteness. I held a session with social work supervisors where we spoke about use of self, and specifically the use of self for positive disruption. When we are faced with those moments of feeling uncomfortable or trepidation when entering a conversation or addressing an issue with a client that had to do with race, think of your higher order purpose. I shared with them that as social workers and especially supervisors, we are guided by a code of ethics that is grounded in social justice. If we can revisit that purpose during these moments that may propel us forward to move outside of ourselves, use ourselves and take what feels like a risk because we have a responsibility to do so.

Discussion Questions

1. In what areas in your professional life are you a leader?
2. Locate yourself as a leader in these areas, what comes up for you?
3. Looking at the organization as a whole, how does leadership communicate the ways that diversity and inclusion is valued at your organization?
4. Does leadership place equal value on diversity and on inclusion?
5. How do leaders create a brave space for their faculty and staff to engage in critical discussions that center race and support another while doing so?
6. Spend time thinking about the difference between authenticity and sincerity. What comes up for you?
7. Finally, locate yourself during the time of COVID-19. What was your process after the murder of Ahmaud Arbery, Breonna

Taylor and George Floyd and the resulting protests? In what ways do you think you have been complicit in systemic racism?

References

Ahmed, S. (2012). *On being included: Racism and diversity in institutional life*. London, UK: Duke University Press.

DuBois, W. E. B. (1903/1963/2003). *The souls of Black folk*. New York, NY: Fine Creative.

Jackson, J. (2005). *Real Black: Adventures in racial sincerity*. Chicago, IL: University of Chicago Press.

Lorde, A. (1983). There is no hierarchy of oppression. *Bulletin: Homophobia and Education*, *14*, 9.

Welang, N. (2018). Triple consciousness: The reimagination of Black female identities in contemporary American culture. *Open Cultural Studies*, 2(1), 296–306.

4

TRANSFORMATIONAL LEADERSHIP

Redefinition

The goal of this project is to positively disrupt the social work field, reconceptualize and broaden the definitions of certain foundational and basic social work terms to consider practice and leadership from a place of trauma-informed inclusion and diversity. All things that should be taught in social work foundation courses. I also recognize, and radically accept, that a full realization of inclusion within the context of the social work classroom and work space may not be completely possible. Much of the success of this work relies on an institutional commitment to social justice, pedagogical practices and professional development. The terms we have thus far unpacked, and reworked are cultural competency, leadership, trauma and trauma-informed practice. The redefinition and re-conceptualization of the terms identified and offered in the previous chapters lends itself to possibility and potential that was not there before. Meaning, these re-conceptualized terms, along with the possibility and potential to work and live in truly inclusive spaces, reside in a framework I would like to call transformational leadership. In this framework, which is also a practice model for social work leadership, there is hope for inclusion and diversity that moves beyond the performative, meaning that diversity and inclusion become more than just an optical phenomenon (Kapuku, 2019). Not only do we see the beauty of diversity in bodies, but we also actively engage in the work of sustaining and integrating that diversity. This requires that spaces are created throughout organizations and in classrooms to unpack and dialogue about the meaning and integration of diversity and inclusion and the social work commitment to social justice. In order for these spaces to be created and sustained, they must be legitimized through formal policy such as in mission statements. When mission statements are created with a shared definition of diversity, and are coupled with an internal look at organizational cultural practices, the statement becomes more than words on paper that look and sound good to the external facing world. Lack of this coupling, renders the mission statement performative. The mission statement performs the act of presenting diversity as a concept without the substance or the rigor involved in the conscious practice of doing the work. The statement becomes language that leaders can stand behind without actually understanding what it means or how to enact it in their leadership. And so, it becomes an idle performance of language because the personal work of locating oneself in these concepts is not part of the act. I have found that the most difficult part of this work lies in the beginning critical conversations. These conversations consist of bringing the organization and teams together to locate themselves as individuals and as a community. In this space, we dialogue about what diversity and inclusion actually means, how each person in their everyday actions, participates in inclusion and exclusion, the impact of the trauma of exclusion and ultimately how to create an environment that is transparent and empathically accountable.

Within this framework of transformational leadership, there is also hope for trauma-informed spaces that are brave and explicitly inclusive. In other words, brave and explicitly inclusive to peel back layers of learnings to unlearn, reconceptualize and dialogue about experiences and topics that go unrecognized and undiscussed in classrooms and traditional organizational cultures. That is, race, racism and white supremacy. In return, the successful creation and utilization of these spaces serves in decreasing stress responses. As discussed in previous chapters, declaring a space, a "safe space," particularly in a culture that may be inherently "unsafe," often does not get to its intended outcome of sincere member engagement and transparency of thought. For example, rhetoric is more likely to be used, generalizations are made and the "elephant" lives in the room. Again, we see how language can serve as a smoke screen and obscure the work needed to create the very spaces to dialogue about traumas that show up in the classroom and in the work space, such as being Black and Brown in predominantly white spaces, microaggressions, social inequities, systemic racism and disparities. These are the traumas that are often not discussed in the classroom and in organizational settings for reasons that may include the denial and lack of recognition of these spaces and acts as actual "traumas," and because of the discomfort, shame and pain that accompany conversions centered around race, inequity and disparity, particularly among white leaders. When such traumas are discussed, there is the likely possibility that the discussion will center around the injured person of color, rather than an explicit look at the normative white organizational culture that these experiences of disparity, inequity and resulting trauma live and grow in. Conversations about race, and in this case the impact of white privilege on organizational cultures, often result in stress and silence, and defensive behaviors among white people (DiAngelo, 2018). In these moments, the felt discomfort and lack of racial stamina among white leaders takes privilege over the stress response felt in Black, Indigenous and people of color who stay silent because the space is not actually "safe." White leaders, including instructors, often fail to interrogate the culture and sit in spaces that acknowledge the impact of and often unconscious participation in the traumas of microaggressions, social inequities and disparities, for example. Black, Indigenous and people of color who stay silent become the victims of these silent traumas as they implicitly hold the responsibility for being the ones pegged to express the concerns relating to the whole Black community. The other possibility in these moments is that a healthy environment is created for Black, Indigenous and people of color to voice their collective traumas but white folks stay silent and opt out of the discussion because of their felt discomfort and shame talking about race, racial traumas and their complicity in upholding systemic racism.

We have now established that labeling something as "safe," does not translate into it being safe. A model of transformational leadership considers the tenets of trauma-informed practice. This means transformational leaders, in practicing inclusion, incorporate physical, spiritual, and emotional safety, choice, collaboration, trustworthiness and empowerment into their model. Instead of seeing inclusion, sometimes termed culturally competent or responsive practice, as an ad-hoc, they see it as central to understanding and practicing the model, and ultimately leading. Understanding and incorporating trauma-informed practice principles through a lens of diversity and inclusion, allows for recognition of traumas that are inclusive of being a Black body in predominantly white spaces and acts of oppression. Looking at and holding the organizational culture empathically accountable for acts of interpersonal and systemic oppression and inequity is very different than being culturally responsive to the needs and experiences of marginalized populations, specifically individuals of color. Transformational leadership from a trauma-informed and diversity and inclusion lens ultimately means re-conceptualizing safety, choice, collaboration, empowerment and trustworthiness in order to deliver services and lead organizations from a lens that is inclusive of the traumas of marginalized populations. Also important in the effectiveness of this approach is recognizing that some of these acts of trauma happen, and will continue to happen, within the same organizational culture that is deemed as "trauma-informed."

Leading from This Lens

How do we use this lens and practice model to lead in spaces that are in our control? The act of leading can take many forms. There are the traditional, fixed leadership roles, such as a head of an agency, organization or a government position, and then there are "spaces" where leadership also shows up. We can lead as social work supervisors, and we can be a leader in such spaces as the classroom, team meetings, interdisciplinary case conferences and in our personal lives with friends and family. Social work leadership has been defined as "the capacity to work creatively, constructively and effectively with individuals, families, groups, organizations and communities to promote social justice, catalyze social change, and address individual and social problems" (Gokhale, K., & Geeta, J. (2015). Simply put, being a leader in the field of social work means motivating people toward change. I re-conceptualized the terms previously identified because this re-conceptualization better aids our efforts toward promoting social justice and social justice is at the core of social work. We cannot work toward change, and social justice, without positively disrupting the status quo; and this same status quo is what defined and created the boundaries around the mis-definitions. Creating an opening in the status quo, and thus in opening up spaces, creates a possibility of true inclusion, whether it be in an organization, classroom setting or public space. This allows for sincere and brave discourse and dialogue. Part of this dialogue requires us to look more deeply at ourselves and why we and that space remains closed to the possibility of true inclusion and a commitment to unlearn and relearn.

Working in the confines and within the boundaries of the traditional definition of "leadership," I am reminded of what transformational leadership is not. I think of those moments in meetings when the possibility of inclusion is lost. Those moments that beg for disruption or acknowledgement and instead the words are left hanging in the air, people shift in their seats, eyes divert away from the person who spoke and leaders quickly move on to the next item on the agenda. A physical stress response is felt. These same tendencies also show up in our classrooms. As a member of meetings, when this happens, I have often wished that an invisible participant observer rang a bell every time we are met with an awkward silence, a comment, question or concern that goes unaddressed, or miss the opportunity to more deeply explore an agenda item that touches on inclusivity, of any kind. I envision not just any bell, but a Buddhist bell of mindfulness and compassion, which would serve as a prop, a physical and positive disruption to help pause, and serve to invite awareness for leaders who are unaware of what was missed. Frequently, when inclusion is not an organization or leadership concern, these moments are approached with hesitation and uncertainty, as acknowledgment involves entering a space of ambiguity. Another common occurrence, is that the organization or leadership is wholly and genuinely unaware of the moment and the potential to intervene. In both of these scenarios an opportunity to build community and deepen the level of engagement with one another is lost. In the first case, it appears that socially constructed notions of traditional leadership and perhaps fear of exposure preside and take over. In the second case, perhaps what we witness is an unconsciousness that is steeped in a particular way of knowing that is binary, myopic and void of mindfulness. A sense of urgency takes over to keep the meeting on task. The complexity of the human condition is overridden. Yet, it is these very moments that are threads to developing, fostering and nurturing sincere relationships that actually serve to move organizations and leaders closer to a safe and inclusive space and culture. This is the work of social justice. I believe in the concept of Revolutionary Love envisioned, created and shared by great leaders such as Che Guevara. Revolutionary Love means a love for humanity. A deep sense of commitment to the fight against oppression, the willingness to sacrifice personal gains and a critical intelligence. This commitment is bigger than the idea of just having feelings of love toward a person, or participating in acts of kindness. Revolutionary Love is not an individual act but rather a love for the pursuit of social justice (McLaren, 2000). These moments during the COVID-19 pandemic and Black Lives Matter movement require choosing love over fear as an act of humanity and social justice. It also requires a deep look at the ideologies that remain unnamed in higher education and in the classroom and the need for positive disruption and reconceptualization.

In my role as an individual coach, or even as a participant observer (I have been asked by executive teams to be that invisible bell ringer inviting a pause or awareness), I ask leaders in all spaces, what stops them from disrupting the flow of the agenda to address what just happened, or even just to sit in the space for a little longer to see what emerges? The answer is usually that they did not know how to address the comment. The need to move on felt more comfortable, more natural, and they were concerned about the time and wanted to make sure to get to every item on the agenda. The other answer I hear a lot, especially if the topic is on race, inequity or disparity is that they felt discomfort and were unsure of what to say and didn't want to say the "wrong" thing. Some even have said, "I did not want to sound racist." Others were unaware that an opportunity even presented itself. The dynamics in the room, the energy and non-verbal communication were denied, unnoticed and unrecognized.

That moment with the leader begs for both compassion and curiosity. Compassion because it is a psychologically hard place to be in knowing that an opportunity was missed and imagining the repercussions of that. Quite often the impact of the felt sense of urgency to "move on" in a meeting cannot be sugar coated with good intention, no matter how noble that intention is, because the intention did not match the impact. At the same time, I want to unpack the constructed notions of "right" and "wrong." These binary notions of right and wrong stop growth, contribute to denial, shame, guilt and lead to stagnation. I wonder about what that fear of vulnerability and exposure of what the leader may not know or may have wrong, feels like for each leader I work with? What are the origins of this fear? What arises in the body when faced with entering a space of ambiguity? What internally comes up for the leader that stops them from diving into a topic or sitting in space that feels uncomfortable? Why is the potential moment for reflection on the psychology of the leader and the training of the leader rejected? For example, the training I sat through on "authentic leadership" did not prepare us for these moments. Neither did the training nor the traditional leadership literature prepare leaders for that terrible feeling that comes with saying something that does not have a positive impact and then challenging that moment into change instead of living in a space of denial or shame. Are leaders taking the time after the meeting, or moment, to sit alone or with a trusted colleague or coach to intentionally and mindfully reflect on what felt uncomfortable and why? What are the origins of this discomfort? We must also acknowledge and confront the socially constructed values of leadership that get in the way, meaning, the need to be "perfect," all-knowing and always certain, the opposite of being vulnerable. In those moments when we worry about saying the "wrong" thing, I wonder what is the right thing to say? The other question that emerges for me is who defines these dichotomous notions of right and wrong? Because it is these very categories of right and wrong that stop leaders from being brave, inclusive, modeling vulnerability and even more essential – being intentionally reflective and introspective. Where is the training and the space to practice being brave and vulnerable with the use of self? The question that surfaces is, if not even leaders themselves feel comfortable enough to disrupt, how can we expect others to? While these questions, that come from a sincere place of curiosity, may be easier for some to ask of themselves then others, the questions are crucial in both unpacking the experience and being able to then re-conceptualize the experience and envision a different outcome. One final question that emerges for me is: are we, as a collective, able to transcend the focus on ourselves? Specifically, can we transcend how we may be perceiving ourselves or be perceived by others in those uncomfortable and ambiguous moments, and instead focus on the mission that drives the organization and the people we serve? I believe this shift in perspective and focus will better position us to enter spaces of uncertainty and ambiguity, and lead from a space of Revolutionary Love.

An effective leader knows how organizations run and a transformational leader has intersectional knowledge of how the organization runs and has intimate knowledge of themselves. The transformational leader does not stand alone in a vacuum of theories and frameworks but actually uses the self to own, locate and push through the felt discomfort. The felt discomfort and lack of decision around how to respond in moments that involve the explicit naming of disparity, inequity and trauma of marginalized groups and in particular Black and Brown staff or students, is in direct contradiction to the traditional role of a leader. The traditional definition and image of a leader is the all-knowing. In traditional leadership theory, self-disconnection is honored as the ability to separate the personal and psychological self from the professional self. In many leadership spaces the ability to compartmentalize is elevated as a leadership skill. Yet, the integration of the self, coupled with the self-compassion needed to live in a leadership space of ambiguity, constant readjustment and sometimes discomfort, is crucial. This self-work transcends to the organizational culture. Leaders able to perform this self-work are then better equipped to challenge and interrogate their current leadership style and practices, its impact on the organizational culture, and ultimately to lead from the heart space. The Socratic claim that an "unexamined life is not worth living," has great merit especially in the context of leadership. This project allows for the opportunity and practice of self-knowledge in ways that have not been elevated in the traditional leadership literature. A practice of getting to know ourselves means engaging in a cultural inventory. It is the ability to locate ourselves, taking an honest, internal and compassionate inventory of the ways our trajectory and life journey impacts our engagement with the foundational terms presented in the previous chapters; cultural competency, trauma, trauma-informed practice and leadership. The ability to continually practice self-reflection and revisit self-location when faced with missed opportunities for inclusion involves some preparatory action steps. These may include but are certainly not limited to, setting intentions and priorities before meetings, making commitments to ourselves to be brave, and having compassion for ourselves and others when we do not see clearly or opt out on (and miss) opportunities for deeper connection and inclusion.

Locating Myself

The skill of learning how to embrace and live through a lens of self-compassion was not innate to me. Thinking about my moments of transformation over time and fraught with much challenge, I have learned to adopt the strategies of compassion for myself and for others.

My journey in self-compassion begins with the work I needed to do in understanding that the death of my brother was not my fault. Learning to instead, have compassion for that 6-year-old girl who happened to be home alone for enough time to find her baby brother blue in his crib. My work in therapy over the years involved, and continues to involve, trauma-informed practices such as Trauma-Informed Cognitive Behavioral Therapy and Eye Movement Desensitization and Reprocessing. Revisiting that little girl with compassion and love instead of blame and hate. My work in the field of trauma in particular with the Seeking Safety curriculum (Najavits, 2002) and with women who had histories of trauma and addiction was a parallel process to my healing.

Self-compassion also showed up in the narrative I had created about living on the margins of multiple identities, that somehow, I was not whole or complete but instead a hodgepodge of cultures without a home and without belonging. I was riding on the coat-tails of socially constructed identities while falling victim to the need for others to box me in and I experienced the accompanying trauma of naming myself in spaces where my identity was divorced. It took time for me to expand the markers of my identity, actively meet people who also occupied this similar space, notice the opportunity in claiming more than one identity, and realize that my identity and sense of belonging was not contingent on how others define me. All of these processes led me to realize that I actually had agency in how I choose to self-identify. I learned that the markers of identity are fluid and nuanced and not easily defined.

Most recently, I am learning to practice self-compassion with my identity as a single mom who has been married and divorced twice. Instead of seeing that as a mark of being "damaged," in a society that holds marriage in high regard, I re-conceptualized this experience to understand it as I do not stay stuck in unhappy situations and when I sense harm to myself or my children, I have the courage to leave.

Professionally, holding compassion at the center of my positive disruptions meant also building community to check things out, process feelings, and make sure I am supported in my efforts and attempts at positive disruption. I reflect on a turning point in my career when I spent the summer teaching at Smith College School of Social Work. I had just received tenure and was transitioning into the position of Associate Dean of Academic Affairs. I had the privilege of attending a seminar by Dean John Jackson from Annenberg School for Communication at the University of Pennsylvania. That night he spoke to a packed house of faculty, students and administrators about the role of love and compassion in his work and in his life. I remember sitting there, exhausted from my own personal struggle and angry at the unearned white advantage, fragility and lack of racial stamina among white folks, including my mother. Further exacerbating this anger and exhaustion of impatience was that my expectations of "Leaders," in this case leaders in the academy, were both high and also not grounded in anything substantial except the title. I care deeply and learned that this caring is also my Achilles heel because when people disappoint me, it cuts deep particularly in professional spaces. From this uncompassionate place, what I now can label as my emotional armor, I questioned Dean Jackson's strategy while also connecting to his words and passion. Knowing that Revolutionary Love and compassion were ultimately a part of my essence and at the root of my work, I winced at the thought that my armor had stopped me from operating from a place of both compassion and sincerity. I left that lecture thinking deeply about my road less traveled, particularly in the leadership space, thinking about who I wanted to be and what exactly was in my way from paying attention to that. That intentional reflection and mindfulness is an ongoing, never-ending, practice that goes hand in hand with locating myself. Working to bring compassion and community building into my life and career, and guiding others to do the same requires an evolved and transformative state of being because leadership is about serving the masses in collaboration with others, not about power hoarding, being served or making up for past traumas.

Tara Brach in her book *Radical Acceptance* speaks about clear seeing and self-compassion as being inseparable (Brach, 2003) and key components in the journey for radical self-acceptance. I pulled Dr. Brach's book off my shelf recently in an attempt to revisit this concept of radical acceptance. I collected and read a number of books during my Masters' program centering on healing, acceptance and mindfulness. If you have not heard of her work or this book in particular, is it worth the read. In considering this project I see mindfulness and compassion as working together to transform social work practice, leaders and leadership spaces. I also recommend the book *My Grandmother's Hands* by Resmaa Menakem (Menakem, 2017). Menakem's work gives voice to the trauma on the Black body and tools to help mend the internalized trauma and pain. The mind body connection is not one that is often centered in traditional social work practice. Courses on mindfulness, meditation, art and film provide a wonderful opportunity to heal in diverse ways that touch the mind, body and spirit. I recently recommended this book to the students in a social work course I teach on trauma. Moving beyond the traditional textbooks to including diverse works of Black, Indigenous and people of color writers is critically important in working toward inclusive spaces.

Transformational Leader Traits

As discussed in the beginning of this chapter, transformational leadership is trauma-informed social work practice through the lens of diversity and inclusion. That is, a re-conceptualization of specific terms to aid in the efforts toward social justice, that begins with the self. My colleague Dr. CarolAnn Daniel reminds me often that when you speak and lead from the heart, nothing can really go wrong. The work lies in locating that heart space and having the courage to share it. I offer these below traits and tools as ways of being and actions that do not cancel out what leaders, educators and students already have in their tool box, but serve as a supplement, and in some cases perhaps a substitute for qualities that do not allow for positive disruption and inclusion. These traits are not to be used as a checklist but instead thoughtfully assessed and then integrated in your leadership practice. Below are some listed traits typically exhibited by those who are transformational leaders. However, it's important to emphasize that in our practice model, leadership is not a rigid structure or feature but dynamic to circumstances and culture. In that vein, these traits build off of one another. Meaning, for example, the trait of being mindfulness is necessary for self-compassion and courage. At this point in the project, let's take some time to talk more explicitly about the traits of a transformational leader.

Read through, and take some time to consider these qualities and assess your readiness to incorporate them into your practice. Remember, do not view them as a checklist but instead, engage with them, meaning, what do each of these qualities mean to you and for you? What challenges come to mind when you think about incorporating these traits into your leadership practice? Below are the details of how I've personally encountered and defined these traits in the social work and leadership fields, all of which are intended to also mitigate the impact of trauma. I consider these leadership traits to be trauma-informed from the lens of diversity and inclusion. All of these traits and tools can be the focus of individual coaching, leadership team meetings and individual supervision. In addition, integrating these traits and tools within foundation social work practice courses by role playing, weekly journal writing and small group exercises and training supervisors to pay attention to how these traits and tools show up or do not show up in process recordings. This would give students the opportunity to practice using themselves and engaging and working with clients through a trauma-informed, diversity and inclusion lens.

Mindfulness

How are you entering spaces? Cultivating a practice of mindfulness means a willingness to live in a state of awareness, free of judgment. How do we cultivate the time and space required to practice mindfulness? Are we able to practice mindfulness and allow for the conscious examination of our reactions and thoughts even when those reactions and thoughts are not positive? Have we fostered a space in our personal lives, organizations, work spaces and classrooms to share our practice of mindfulness with others?

Personally, I have found that so much of my life has operated from a reactionary place. However, it was not until I was ready and willing to commit to a practice of mindfulness, that this became apparent to me. I found that I often felt, and feel, the need to respond and behave from a defensive place without first taking the time to self-examine where those feelings are coming from. I often used my life story and copy it as a template for others, and would become incredibly disappointed when they did not meet my expectations. Other examples include rushing to respond to an email without first thinking about my intention and the potential impact of my message, entering a supervisory session, meeting space or a class without first setting an agenda for myself and practicing some self-care, and waking up each morning in a rush to start the day without first striving to write down my thoughts in a free association fashion in a journal, free of judgment. These practices serve as a purging for me to allow for new ideas and ways of being to enter my mind. To be clear – my commitment to my practice of mindfulness ebbs and flows. There are days that I wish I were more consistent, but the reality is that there are moments when life is overwhelmingly busy or I just do not feel like being mindful in that particular moment. I think the difference now is that I strive to accept all of those moments without judgment too. I also have those people in my life who help me work through difficult moments. Specifically, I have had colleagues become close friends who I can check in with after meetings and classes to see how I could have been more mindful and to help me take a deeper look at myself and what exactly I may have been reacting to in the moment. Who are these people in your life? Or who in your life has the potential to be that person? Cultivating a system of support especially when leading an organization feels crucial.

In this project, mindfulness is first about locating yourself in the moment of your practice and leadership. My personal practice has been to sit quietly with a pen and paper and locate myself. Journal writing has been a great tool for me. Perhaps you can find something equivalent? Starting with the first introduction to our histories and life trajectories and what led us to this moment of leadership. As the practice of mindfulness becomes more intentional and normative, awareness begins to grow. For example, perhaps in the past you may have not noticed a pause in a meeting that begged for interrogation, but now with more centering you begin to notice more and your awareness begins to grow. Mindfulness in an organization setting also means being conscious and aware of the diverse bodies in the room, in the meeting and in the classroom. Who is sitting where, who talks the most, who remains quiet? It is important to check in with folks in the beginning and close with time remaining to ensure that there is space and time to re-enter whatever environment they are returning to. Essentially, mindfulness is the willingness to open up space in your mind to consider and attend to all there is to attend to, not just what feels comfortable and familiar.

Self-Compassion and Compassion for Others

Self-compassion is one of the most difficult traits to practice, especially in a society that does not lend itself to kindness, forgiveness and healing. The undergird philosophy of Puritan-Rugged Individualism carries with it a narrative that the self-sufficient individual is better off, and preferable. We see a focus on individual blame and unworthiness rather than an interrogation of the structural inequalities that are responsible for much of the disparity and inequity across racial lines. Coupled with this philosophy are the social constructions of gender, in particular masculinity. Asking for example, a male identified leader to be a compassionate leader in the face of the confines of philosophical Puritan and Capitalistic teachings coupled with the constructions of gender is a heavy ask. For leaders of color, this ask is even more difficult because it requires a level of vulnerability and unmasking that can be tricky.

Compassion is an action that needs to be practiced and nurtured, but before this it must be a trait that is valued. When we see compassion as a trait that is constructed as a "soft" skill or connotes a sense of weakness, then time is not allotted to practice it. I have seen a plethora of articles on the Internet that speak to how to be a compassionate leader but I am not sure it is an achievable if the trait itself is not valued, seen as a strength, supported and internalized.

I learned a lot about self-compassion through my early work with women who have histories of trauma and substance abuse. The work involved teaching women to have compassion for themselves, rather than shaming themselves for traumas that happened to them, and traumas they had no control of. We spent entire weeks on teaching the skills of self-compassion and asking for help (Najavits, 2002). Among the lessons learned was the realization that the women did the best they could at the time, and that coping with their traumas by numbing their pain with alcohol and other substances was the only way they knew how to get rid of the emotional and physical pain. For many, positive coping and asking for help was not an option. Are there examples you can think of personally or professionally where you could have had more compassion for yourself?

What got in the way of self-compassion? How would you have treated yourself differently if you had the opportunity to revisit that moment?

In moments where self-compassion and compassion are necessary, like the COVID-19 pandemic, we try to navigate the many traumas and constantly readjust. There is a rawness and vulnerability that begs for compassion in ourselves and in others. In this model of leadership, compassion begins with the self and then extends to others. Compassion sits right alongside mindfulness in being able to create or find a sincere place of healing within and for ourselves that can literally transcend to others. Mindfulness coupled with compassion allows us, from the heart, to positively disrupt spaces while also having compassion for others who choose not to or do not know how to make room for others. Compassion shows up in the ability to hold space for everyone. Meaning, the compassion for the pain from exclusion among Black, Indigenous and people of color and the compassion for white leaders who struggle with a critical racial analysis and have unknowingly or knowingly practiced exclusion. It is one thing to understand compassion and then another to make room and time to commit to the work involved with practicing compassion.

Comfortable With Nuance

In this project, being comfortable with nuance as a leader means being able to recognize and then hold the complexity and multiple experiences of staff, colleagues and students all at once. This is a process that disrupts the binary ideology. That is, the ability to recognize nuance first and then be comfortable with expanding the lens and finally making the time to hold and work with nuance. Nuance is the rejection of dualist thinking and of binary opposites. I see being comfortable with nuance as a requirement for leading in diverse environments that are innately fluid and dynamic because you notice the details of a person and the details of experience. A fixed mindset that desires to simplify, for any number of reasons, does not allow for the awareness or recognition of subtle similarities and differences that are always present in race, culture, religion and gender. Therefore, a fixed mindset cannot possibly allow for sincere diversity or inclusion. Understanding that identities cannot be conflated and that there is for example, a difference between Black and African American, that all Latinx cultures and ethnicities are not the same, or that the Asian Diaspora is incredibly expansive. Nuance often gets lost or undervalued in crisis driven environments, yet it is the nuance of person and approach that allows for true integration and the beauty of diversity. Nuance is a more sophisticated approach to leadership that entails taking the time to notice the variation in people. In fact, I would say that nuance is necessary because without it, generalizations and assumptions are made based on the dominate discourse that is grounded in particular ways of knowing. One question to ask yourself is when we desire to simplify someone or something who or what gets excluded by that simplification?

Courage

The journey to being courageous is dynamic and very much in line with the social work person-in-environment framework. Social workers help clients become more courageous as they begin to heal and substitute positive coping for negative coping. The act of deciding to heal is a courageous act. You may find that you have courage in some areas compared to others. Have compassion for yourself if you notice that this is the case. Practice mindfulness to better understand what evokes fear in some spaces as opposed to others.

What areas in your life do you feel courageous? Personally, I find that I have so much courage in my role as a mother. I see myself able to take risks and have conversations with my children. I have courage in my consulting work with my clients and with my students in the classroom to ask the hard questions and hold them empathically accountable, challenging them to dig deeper than they thought they could. I have less courage in some of my interpersonal relationships. I am mindful that my history of trauma and exclusion has dampened my courage in this arena, so my work has been to draw on those areas where I do have courage and use that as a model for self-integration of courage.

Creating brave spaces requires courage. Courage can take the internal form of starting and committing to the act of self-location and also the outward act of speaking your truth. Transformational leadership means an awareness and understanding of ones' positionality, courage in addressing power dynamics, and a focus on relationship building. To be more prepared to facilitate a brave conversation, in the workplace, about diversity, inclusion and equity dynamics in your interactions and relationships at work takes courage. Can you recall a time when you could have entered a space braver than you did? What stopped you and how would you do it differently if the opportunity arises again?

Vulnerability

Vulnerability deepens the connection to ourselves and our work. Allowing ourselves to be seen gives permission for others to also do the same. Vulnerability takes courage. It takes courage to share ourselves in ways that may be very different from how we were taught to, particularly in a leadership space. Transformational leadership requires a relationship to self and other where one can be vulnerable and forthcoming without fear of judgement. It requires both diligence and consistency over a long period of time. The work shows up in meetings and informal interactions, trainings are artificial settings where material can be transported but the "how to," in real life settings is missing. I have found Brené Brown's (Brown, 2018) research on vulnerability and her book *Dare to Lead* as a great resource to work on and incorporate vulnerability into my own practice. Brown has exercises in her book that allow for the practice of vulnerability in personal arenas and in organizational settings.

Empathic Accountability

I see the trait of accountability as something that is generous. My understanding of accountability is that people care enough about me and my work to make sure I am honoring my commitments, whatever they are. As a leader, I am working with my clients to ensure they too are honoring their commitments through their behaviors and their actions. Yet, I understand that many do not hold themselves accountable and instead see this word, and any action attached to it, more like scrutiny. I remember sitting in a faculty meeting and making a request along the lines of how I wish we were a community where we were able to hold each other accountable, without defensiveness or judgment, to better meet the needs of our diverse student body. That request alone was met with so much defensiveness from a white male colleague, as if I had just accused him of something. It is for this reason that I couple the words empathic with accountability.

How do you build an organization that is grounded in a mission of social justice without a level of accountability? What I like to call empathic accountability. This means, holding leaders accountable for their commitment to diversity, equity and inclusion. This may look like supporting them with the help of individual coaching, and creating internal measures like performance reports and a feedback loop. These supports help better understand how colleagues are working toward this goal of empathetic accountability, *personally within themselves* and within the organization. A culture of accountability allows for automatic checks and balances to ensure the integrity of the mission. At the same time, accountability measures must be balanced. Often times we see that some folks are held more accountable then others, particularly in organizations with fewer Black, Indigenous and people of color. Whether this is because of bias or nepotism, the feedback should be consistent, equitable and purposeful. Otherwise, the hope of sincere accountability for the good of the mission is lost.

Curiosity

Are you curious about your actions, thoughts and behaviors? I have always believed that we can teach curiosity and that using curiosity as a tool allows for the opening up of spaces for oneself and for others. Think about it, there is so much power in the asking of a question. There is also an opportunity to build community because we learn about one another by asking questions. Yet, I have found in my personal and professional life that in general, folks are more likely to assume rather than ask a question. How often do you honor curiosity? How often do you fall back on your own personal assumptions instead of risking the ask? When I ask these questions and offer such observations in a professional setting, that is, that we are more likely to assume then ask a question, the response is something like, "I did not want to offend the person by asking." Yet, the irony in that response is how does anyone know what someone else finds offensive? We assume, because asking the question makes us uncomfortable, that the person receiving the question will also be uncomfortable. We rarely take the risk to check our assumption out and instead stay stuck in our narratives assuming we know, or in some cases, being comfortable with not knowing. Of course, I gather we all can cite examples of evidence of past behavior when asking any question may just elicit the same response, but those are not the times I am talking about. I am talking about those moments of potential sincere inquiry that could lead to a deeper relationship, a deeper more engaged community but instead we do not ask. Academics are in the business of language, and with that comes many different ways of understanding and interpreting words. I find myself asking such phrases as, "can you tell me more," "what does that mean to you," and "I am not sure I understand, can you give me an example?" Not taking a statement at face value is also a way to educate. Again, imploring the skills of both a clinician and qualitative researcher in an effort to probe, find understanding and in some cases, shared meaning. There is a humanity and humility to honoring curiosity because it allows you to know and learn what you did not know.

Trauma Responsive

All of the leadership traits listed above help leaders create organizational cultures that are trauma responsive. In this particular leadership model being a trauma responsive leader means expanding the trauma lens to also include the traumas of everyday oppressions and then, being responsive to how these traumas may be re-created within the organizational culture, within the classroom or within the training or workshop. I think of the hierarchy in an organization when we see the majority of the direct service staff as Black, Indigenous and people of color but not placed in positions to influence policy, the recruitment process, the messaging, the acknowledgement and celebration of holidays, gender neutral bathrooms; all of which fall under the heading of being trauma responsive. The organization or the classroom should ideally operate as a sanctuary from the everyday realities of the outside world.

Reflection

Leadership is an opportunity to serve others and an opportunity to serve ourselves. Now more than ever we see a need for this kind of transformational leadership, particularly in the field of social work. A type of leadership that starts from self-location and considers how our various life experiences and identities show up in our leadership, understanding that leadership takes many forms and is a fluid and dynamic space. Social works commitment to a person-in-environment framework includes not just the client in the environment, but the social worker as well. The use of self is also a dynamic process that requires mindful readjustment and reflection. Social workers are often taught this practice skill of use of self in the beginning of their formal school training and then do not bother to apply it in later courses, or once beginning to practice. Not only does the use of self sometimes stop, but it remains void of the use of self to positively disrupt normative spaces. There is an opportunity right now to take risks with ourselves and others that we have not before and centering mindfulness, self-compassion and compassion for others, nuance, courage, vulnerability, empathic accountability, curiosity and trauma responsiveness, which ultimately aids toward building community, healing and diversity and inclusion

---

Discussion Questions

1. Reflect on this chapter and the questions that were raised. Can you identify moments in meetings or in a classroom setting where you consciously chose not to enter a space of ambiguity and uncertainty? Can you locate what you felt, where you felt it in your body and what stopped you from speaking up?

2. If you could revisit those moments, how would you have done it differently?
3. Next to each leadership trait I identified write down ways you already practice that trait and ways you could do better? Which traits feel more difficult to integrate?
4. How would you use these also as tools for your practice?

References

Brach, T. P. (2003). *Radical acceptance: Embracing your life with the heart of a Buddha*. New York, NY: Bantam.

Brown, B. (2018). *Dare to lead*. New York, NY: Random House.

DiAngelo, R. (2018). *White fragility*. Boston, MA: Beason Press.

Gokhale, K., & Geeta, J. (2015). *Leadership: An important domain in social work education. Social Work Footprints*. Available at https://www.socialworkfootprints.org/english-articles/leadership-an-important-domain-in-social-work-education

Kapuku, R. (2019, September 3). Why performative diversity agendas are failing the most marginalised communities. *Medium*, p. 1. Available at https://medium.com/@reneekapuku/why-performative-diversity-agendas-are-failing-the-most-marginalised-communities-aaff56024b14

McLaren, P. (2000). *Che guevara, Paulo Freire, and the pedagogy of revolution*. Lanham: Rowman and Littlefield.

Menaken, R. (2017). *My Grandmother's hands: Racialized trauma and the pathway to mending our hearts and our minds*. Las Vegas, NV: Central Recovery Press.

Najavits, L. (2002). *Seeking safety: A treatment manual for PTSD and substance abuse*. New York, NY: Guildford Press.

5

CHALLENGES TO TRANSFORMATIONAL LEADERSHIP

The chapter we just concluded was heavy in reflection. Reflection in terms of your social work practice, your own leadership style and how that style supports, challenges or falls somewhere in the middle of our concept of Transformational Leadership. Ideally, you also took the time to reflect on the identified traits of mindfulness, self-compassion and compassion for others, nuance, courage, vulnerability, empathic accountability, curiosity and trauma responsiveness. Consider your personal assessment of these traits and how each one can be better integrated into your personal and professional practices.

Personal Challenges

I am curious if during those moments of reflection in the past chapter, and as you have utilized these reflective practices in your everyday life, you, the reader, were also able to locate and then think more deeply about of all the reasons why you, at times, may be unable to operate from a transformational lens? Meaning, were you able to identify some personal challenges and barriers to becoming a Transformational Leader? The obstacles you identified could be the result of a number of factors including; your education, the environment, your training, where you are in your individual growth, and the ways you may have adopted more of the traditional leadership traits and consciously stayed within spaces that looked similar to you. I have noticed in my work that these are usually some of the barriers present that prevent the social worker and leader I'm working with from taking the next step. There may have been moments during your reading of Chapter 4 when the challenges and responses you identified came from a place of armor and defensiveness. This may look like "excuses," or a complete denial or dismissal of the material presented. One way to turn these barriers into productive forces toward transformational leadership is to first acknowledge them. Next, unpack the blockage and look more deeply at the origins of the response. This is an opportunity to practice mindfulness and "notice without judging," in order to locate yourself in the moment when you began to "react" to, instead of consider, the material. As discussed earlier, we generally see and respond to the world through our individual lens that is grounded in our personal histories and ways of knowing. Any interruption of this way of knowing may feel uncomfortable. Yet, when we hold onto our epistemologies and constructions of our identities so tight, we constrict ourselves literally and figuratively. As a result, we may miss opportunities to expand our lens, thus blocking or obstructing our ability to engage with different ways of being and knowing, in this case, specific to social work practice and leadership. It may also limit how we see and respond to others and how we connect with the trait and tool of compassion. What might it feel like to let go a little? For some this is a liberating process, for others this is a process that is fraught with uncertainty, ambiguity and fear, and perhaps a mixture of all of the above for some. Any transition into the unfamiliar brings emotional and psychological challenges. Yet, the practice of social justice is one of liberation; liberation of the mind, body and spirit.

What we now look to do is assess your comfort level with this approach to social work practice and leadership. The next necessary step in order to integrate this material into our practice is identifying personal challenges and barriers to implementation. The focus on personal challenges moves us away from the "checklist" approach, to a deeper engagement with the material, with ourselves and the emotional impact of the material in a sincere way. Thus far, I have worked and continue to work with social work supervisors, heads of Human Resource and CEOs who have been incredibly successful from an organizational standpoint in their roles as leaders, yet have so much trepidation about how to use themselves in areas of diversity, equity and inclusion, and how to sincerely connect with clients and staff of color. It is so much easier and natural for them to craft a mission statement, plan a large event or bring in a speaker then it is for them to speak from the heart and be vulnerable particularly when speaking about race, racism and whiteness. Much of my coaching and our dialogues involve the importance of messaging and taking the opportunity to communicate the value of this work in sustained and consistent ways. The tone of the message, the language used and the action steps communicated are essential in any message. This means working with the leader to find opportunities to instill the importance of diversity, equity and inclusion in everyday practices, not just as a reaction to times of crisis or acknowledgment of holidays. It also means asking white leaders to be vulnerable about the internal work that they are simultaneously doing. Some examples of messaging include, weekly newsletters with a section devoted to inclusion, always having inclusion on the agenda in meetings, sharing personal stories and being vulnerable to talking about the difficulty of this work from their social location. When developing this messaging, questions from leaders include; will I sound defensive, angry or insincere? Will I offend? In our coaching session, we spend time unpacking the feelings and the rhetoric in order to get to the underlining message of what exactly they want to say and how to be vulnerable in that messaging. Often times, the coaching session transitions to personal experiences of inclusion or exclusion and familial stories of race, religion and gender. Through our relationship, they are able to take more risks by sitting in moments of silence, making mistakes, adopting different ways of knowing and leading and over time, the messaging becomes more consistent and more vulnerable.

Opportunities for Positive Disruption

Once we locate ourselves in our personal challenges we can think more strategically about how to better recognize and seize the opportunity to disrupt our ways of knowing and behaving. There are opportunities to do this such as formal education, entering careers for the first time and career advancement. First-year college students, transfer students, first semester master students and doctoral students enter into new. These environments are opportunities for positive disruption. White students, students of color, LGBTQ+ students and international students enter a diverse and complex environment and are confronted with difference in community and intellectual rigor that often challenges the many facets of identity that they have held close for so long. As instructors we have the privilege to assist students in their personal evolution as they navigate the new and different college terrain, ideally, with the goal of becoming lifelong learners. Think back to my example of my first class in my Masters' of Social Work program. My professors' response to my confession of why I wanted to pursue a Masters in Social Work was a jarring and transformational moment that shifted my identity and ways of knowing through positive disruption. Accepting this moment, as something positive instead of punitive, took courage and vulnerability. Accepting this moment allowed me to learn from this disruption and welcome the opportunity to shift. Let's briefly return to your personal moments of reflection. Accepting moments where you identified barriers or past excuses that make you feel guilty or uncomfortable can actually be a productive force. When we are able to accept these moments that initially feel punitive, we are able to let go of old ways of knowing and shift our focus to a sincere heart space that may be more aligned with our purpose. Accepting these moments also allows us to expand in ways we may not even be aware of.

Another example of a transition that brings with it the potential for disruption and personal evolution is the move into a leadership position in an organization. However, how one personally navigates career advancement is crucial. An advancement to a leadership position in an agency is an opportunity for white leaders in particular, to disrupt systems. For leaders of color, the playing field is not as open to facilitate change due to real and felt precarity. In fact, moves up the ladder may serve to unveil the organization's normalization of whiteness in both body, practice and ideology. Tema Okun and Kenneth Jones created a document called *The Characteristics of White Supremacy Culture* (Okun & Jones, 2001). I offer this document to organizations I work with as a way to help them assess and name the dominant white organizational culture. This document serves as a guide to take a closer look at which behaviors and standards are valued, rewarded and communicated. What are the organizational norms? Does everyone know that these are the norms? Are these norms grounded in an ideology of white supremacy? Is there room to offer new and different ways of being? I recently spoke with Tema to thank her for her work and to find out more about the origins of this document. Tema's document highlights the characteristics of white supremacy culture that are used as standards, norms and ways of being based on her and her colleagues' practice experience. I encourage you to visit the site called *Dismantling Racism* and take a look at this document and her other work. The White Supremacy Organizational Characteristics include; perfectionism, sense of urgency, defensiveness, quantity over quality, worship of the written word, the belief that there is only one right way, paternalism, valuing either-or thinking, power hoarding, fear of open conflict, individualism, belief that "I'm" the only one who can do this right, progress is associated with bigger-more, objectivity and right to comfort. For every characteristic she has an antidote that offers a different way of operating. The antidotes push back against white supremacy culture. For example, instead of operating from a sense of urgency, realistic work plans are established and decisions are made with the lens of diversity and inclusion. All of the antidotes that are offered speak to a sincere engagement with diversity and inclusion at every level of the organization. Often times, leaders, especially white leaders, don't even realize that these characteristics and traits are rooted in white supremacy. The mere fact that the document names this and brings it to the leader's attention makes it a very valuable resource. Naming in itself can be a difficult and invaluable practice, coupled with the antidotes provided, this document becomes vital for my practice of consulting.

White Organization Culture in Practice

The white organizational values and practices mentioned above run counter to a trauma-informed, diverse and inclusive style of social work practice and leadership and can serve as barriers to its implementation. I see these practices play out in my experience at the university and within organizations. For example, perfectionism falls heavy on executive leadership. I have seen this practice predominantly in white women leaders. In the relationships I build with women in the leadership space, I have come to understand that the felt pressure for white woman, in particular in leadership, is very intense. Couched in a patriarchal society that devalues women in general, the drive toward perfectionism is real. In the non-profit world, some have come from other for-profit organizations that were male dominated and have fought very hard to move up the ranks and make it into a leadership position. These moves required a use of self that was driven toward perfectionism. However, the pressure white women put on themselves to be "perfect" within the white and male space was carried over and felt internally throughout the agency. The lens of perfectionism is often deficit focused instead of strength based. There is little time made for reflection on the process because the behavior is grounded by a need to "get it right." This leads to a lack of collaboration, a central trauma-informed tenet, and a culture that feels heavy, punitive and driven by a self-fulfilling prophecy to be perfect in the eyes of others while also yearning for validation and praise. I have worked with women who connect this need for perfection back to their former jobs, being a woman in a patriarchal society and childhood experiences. Through coaching they are able to identify how and when it shows up in their leadership. Perfectionism always falls short and leaves many leaders with a psychological gap that cannot be filled by the social construction of what "leadership" means to them. Other ways perfectionism shows up is that there is little time, energy or money put into reflection or identifying lessons learned that can improve practice, meaning, little or no learning from mistakes. There is the tendency to identify what's wrong and little ability to identify, name and appreciate what is right.

The other characteristic that surfaces a lot is the sense of urgency. The need to act without collaboration or thought and often times from a place of anxiety. The sense of urgency drives behavior and leaves little room for inclusion, and the empowerment of others through collaboration. Trust erodes after time as the doubt of being included in "the process" surfaces. The work within organizational departments becomes siloed and leaves little room to build community or feel a part of the process. This sense of urgency is palpable and feels chaotic. Hiring decisions, messaging, meetings and projects constructed from a sense of urgency leave people excluded and feeling left out of the process. Within this value and behavior of urgency is the great potential for implicit bias. Meaning, leaders are operating from a place that feels familiar and comfortable and often racially comfortable. Within that space there is the potential to work out of implicit assumptions based on race, gender and culture.

Fear of open conflict also runs counter to the core tenets of trauma-informed practice. Organizations have values that speak to this notion of "safe" spaces; however, there remains a defensiveness when feedback is given and received, particularly if there is an element of power within the relationship. Employees and supervisees ask, do I have the authority to question my manager or supervisor? The traditional and ingrained hierarchical relationship in leadership does not allow for open conflict. Conflict is viewed not as generous or as an opportunity to see something from a different lens, but rather as a questioning of power and authority that often becomes personal. In my social work foundation courses, I spend a lot of time on this notion of conflict by helping students understand how they personally engage with conflict and the impact on their practice. We unpack the implications of being conflict adverse in their personal lives and how that impacts the relationship with their clients. Fear of open conflict minimizes the opportunities to have brave and critical conversations. Providing opportunities to model working through conflict is particularly important for leaders and for social workers in their work with clients. Role playing anticipated conflicts is one of the antidotes to fear of open conflict that Tema and Kenneth discuss (Okun, *Dismantaling Racism*). When an organizational culture lives in a fear of open conflict, the workspace and relationships are constricted. Fear of conflict does not allow for the empathic accountability needed to move the needle to a more inclusive and equitable climate, not does it build a diverse community.

In my immediate work following the reinvigoration of the Black Lives Matter movement that ensued following the murders of Ahmaud Arbery, Breonna Taylor and George Floyd I saw these white organizational traits and behaviors come to life. It was as if organizations regressed in order to try to gain control of the situation. Once they realized they could not, they began to let go and open up the space little by little. Forums had to be created to allow for employees to voice their pain, shame and name actions steps to addressing systemic racism. The organizations and universities who did this from a heart space were more successful in the forums. Meaning, employees came together to hold the pain for one another and talk directly and transparently about ways the organization can move forward toward a place of inclusion and equity. Leaders attended these sessions and also shared their pain in the case of leaders of color and for white leaders' ways they are working to better understand their denial of complicity in upholding systemic racism and ways to do better both for themselves and for leaders in their organizations.

In some instances, movement into a leadership position requires a reverence to such identified norms, standards and ways of being that are not diverse or inclusive, but are nonetheless valued and rewarded. Assuming a leadership position in an organization can lead to a kind of indoctrination into norms and standards valued by the dominated white group. I have worked with executive leadership teams and have witnessed the process of group think and the adherence to a white supremacy culture. This type of system inhibits, or altogether does not allow for, the expression of difference or diversity of thought. I am reminded specifically of an all-white executive leadership team that professed the desire to be guided by a mission of diversity, equity and inclusion. I was hired to facilitate a day-long workshop but when the time came to think more deeply about how the organizational culture and leadership may be based on a white supremacy model, the white and male leader became defensive and a few white women members on the team who previously seemed to be open to looking more closely at the culture, shut down. Needless to say, I was politely thanked for the day of service, but not invited to work with the organization on a long-term basis. Therein lies the potential for positive disruption with the unintended impact of trauma, specifically for non-dominate groups who challenge the existing organizational culture and bring a different perspective and style to the work space. Here we can think back to my experience in an Associate Dean position. I chose to forgo my opportunities for leadership because in this space I learned that, for me, the trauma of disruption that I experienced outweighed the opportunity for leadership in the academy at this point in my career. We see in these examples that we have choices and ultimately, your willingness to take a risk and capitalize on moments, which beg for positive disruption, will, in part, determine your effectiveness as a transformational leader. What are these risks for you? Perhaps the risks felt different at different and in different contexts. This chapter acknowledges, validates and discusses the challenges with holding and working from a transformational lens to the leadership space.

Locating Myself

I'd like to turn now to locating myself in this discussion of risks and how risks show up differently in different spaces and in different contexts. The risks deserve a constant unpacking using the tools and traits just mentioned. When environments become more transparent, brave and collaborative spaces where mindfulness, compassion, courage, vulnerability, curiosity and accountability are modeled by leadership, the risk to speak one's truth diminishes. Risk continues to diminish when we are able to change with the environment, meaning, investing in coaching or therapy to better our understanding of our triggers in order to speak our truth. Speaking one's truth may take the form of positive disruption.

Personally, this discussion brings me back to my re-entry to a faculty position after stepping away from the role of Associate Dean. When I returned to my Associate faculty role, despite the fact that I had tenure, I was fearful of speaking my truth. This showed up in faculty meetings, smaller committee meetings and even seeped into the classroom. Through the process of reflecting, supportive talks with close friends and colleagues and the passing of time, I connected this fear to the environment. Through this process of reflecting, I came to the realization that this fear was cultivated by the organizational culture, and the fact that I had given away my power of self-definition and confidence in myself and my higher order purpose. My previous experience in leadership was so traumatizing that returning to faculty felt like a relapse. Having worked in the field of addictions and trauma for quite some time, I have always been drawn to the phrase that relapse is part of recovery. When we relapse in behavior or thought, we have a chance to identify the trigger or triggers that initiated that relapse. Identifying, understanding and working through those triggers, becomes part of the recovery process. The idea is that the rate of relapse decreases as you come to a place of self-compassion during those moments of relapse, and are able to better understand the triggers and the behaviors and thought processes associated with those triggers. The ways in which I was triggered by the actions of white and male leadership when I was in that position, caused a relapse in my thought process and in my behaviors. Instead of seeing the system and leadership as dysfunctional, I internalized it. It brought me back to a younger time when I was fearful of raising my hand in class for fear of exposure that I had the wrong answer, it ignited feelings of imposter syndrome, brought back memories of being ridiculed for not being a good test taker, and most recently, created the constant felt need to validate my self-worth, value and intellect as a woman of color in academy. The risk was a psychological one that weighted heavy on my ability to own my "stuff," as my colleague Dr. Rani Varghese said, and speak my truth. Furthermore, I was angry a lot, punching holes in the system, remaining silent, expression disruption only internally, with the exception of close colleagues.

However, two things began to happen at the same time, the environment changed and I returned to therapy. The first was that there were enough disruptions in the system by others that there was a change in leadership. Yet this change alone did not make it much easier for me to risk speaking my truth. Even with the new leadership, at that time, I had not fully come to understand my psychological relapse in my behaviors and thoughts. In fact, it took several months after leadership changed hands, for me to slowly began to enter the system again and "own my stuff," speak my truth and positively disrupt spaces. Part of this process in returning to my old self, included work in therapy that helped me see and face my triggers. What is interesting about this process is that as my practice of mindfulness increases, I am able feel in my body when I am triggered and physically witness my anxiety, which for me shows up in my stomach. In these moments I breathe, recognize what is happening and usually end up speaking. For me, this happens a lot in faculty meetings particularly when I notice that diversity, inclusion and social justice are not honored in curricula, leadership styles and student experiences. Once I notice what is happening to me and what the trigger is, the hesitation to speak up dissolves. I try to think of my higher order purpose, and strive to have no expectation of the outcome or need for validation for whatever I may be contributing to the conversation in that moment. I am more successful now then I have been, and it is a constant practice.

Professional Challenges

Below is a list of challenges that work to potentially inhibit our ability to lead from a transformational lens. This is not an exhaustive list. The list is comprised from my own work with executives and my own personal experience.

Precarity

Precarity is a challenge that may inhibit the ability to lead from a transformational lens. I remember a workshop I facilitated for an organization. This particular training was for a university and so the participants were a mixture of faculty and administration. Demographically, they were a diverse group in terms of age, gender, culture, race and religion. The topic of the training was conscious inclusion, with some attention paid to implicit bias and microaggressions. I modeled vulnerability from the onset by sharing stories of my experiences in professional arenas, my experiences growing up, and ways I have had to disrupt systems, including my family, to be more inclusive. I spoke about the challenges and fears that came with that. After everyone introduced themselves, they made a list of shared commitments for our time together and engaged in a collaborative discussion on implicit bias and microaggressions. I then separated them into small groups. I find that small group work allows for a deeper engagement with the work, as well as the opportunity for increased intimacy and connection among group members. One of the questions that they had to consider in the small group discussion was, what stops them from speaking their truth when they witness or directly experience an act of implicit bias or a microaggression? After about 15 minutes, we gathered back together as a large group and everyone reported back. Once we had everyone back together, we discussed the previous question in this larger setting; what stops folks from speaking up in various spaces on issues of social justice? When probed, a participant shared that *precarity* was the reason why they did not speak up. That is, they were fearful of being demoted, fired or retaliated against if they were to challenge the organizational culture or question their supervisor. The participant shared that the organizational culture did not lend itself to traits such a curiosity or vulnerability and so as a result, they remained silent and discontented. *Even though this person was in a position of leadership within their department*, they did not feel secure enough in their employment to positively disrupt any space, even if they noticed that conversation and resulting actions from the conversation were not aligned with the organization's commitment to social justice. Furthermore, the few times issues regarding diversity, equity and inclusion were raised, they were raised by Black, Indigenous and people of color and the conversation fell flat. Various members of the group supported her statement and offered similar sentiments as it related to their own departments. Although no one had actually ever been fired for speaking up, there was no evidence that the organization supported or valued disruption. The lack of explicit support around disruption was enough to give leaders feelings of precarity even though no one has been fired. Not firing people for speaking up is not enough, especially when examples of disruption are not abundant. This is an example of the difference between being not racist and anti-racist. The organization may not have fired people for speaking up but the white and normative status quo was maintained by not modeling, supporting or encouraging disruption (Kendi, 2019). In addition, the leadership was primarily made up of white males and so it felt even more risky to "call out" incidents of implicit bias or microaggressions because of the lack of visual representation of women and Black, Indigenous and people of color. What resulted was a lack of morale and a distrust in the system to stand behind the organizations' social justice mission.

Another example of precarity's impact on diversity and inclusion that I have heard in my work is the fear of losing funding from donors who are not aligned with missions of social justice. In this example, a Black male CEO of a non-profit organization disregarded any felt precarity and vulnerability, and took up the presented opportunity to disrupt, only to lose out on a potential funding source. He shared with me that he challenged the leader of a major foundation who talked about diversity but could not explain why the foundation did not employ any program officers who were individuals of color, even though the program officers were the people who make the recommendations for funding. Needless to say, the CEO did not receive any financial support from the foundation. In this example, he took the risk to honor curiosity, empathically hold him accountable and disrupt the funder's commitment to diversity and inclusion. When he did, he did not get the support he needed.

Think about the emotional toll that comes with constantly weighing the risks and opportunities in giving voice to disparity and inequity, particularly for leaders of color and for women. There is precarity in being vulnerable in organizations when you are not the majority. As leaders of color and women in predominately white and male spaces, vulnerability is risky. Meaning, the cultural norms are not such where vulnerability is seen as a strength instead of a weakness. Furthermore, the social constructions of race and gender make it very difficult to operate from a place of vulnerability and not fear that those shared experiences will be held against you or that you will be viewed as less then or pitied. There is a fine line between empathy and sympathy. What amplifies the precarity of vulnerability even more, is the historical legacy of racism and anti-Blackness, and the resultant racial inequities and social constructions of Blackness in America. In this case, vulnerability feels like exposure to a system that does not look like you or actively support efforts toward including those who look like you in the decision-making process. My Black female colleague at another institution shared that even as a tenured Chair of her department, she is risk averse particularly when it comes to owning her work and sharing her scholarship in public spaces at the university because she fears standing out in front, alone and unsupported.

Precarity manifests in palpable and diverse ways. We cannot assume that leaders are inherently equipped with the tools to consider the many ways that precarity shows up. The traditional traits and tools associated with leadership do not uphold mindfulness as a valued trait or as a crucial part of social work practice. Yet, there is a need for learning and practicing mindfulness in order to notice precarity. This brings us back to the need to first locate ourselves. Locating ourselves allows us to better understand how we are engaging with the principles of trauma-informed practice through the lens of diversity and inclusion. One outcome of this is increased awareness in noticing how we lead, where our attention goes and where precarity is manifested in organizational culture. How are we as leaders benefiting and contributing to precarity? How can we create kind enough communities to minimize precarity and allow for braver spaces for leaders and those who they lead to be vulnerable? Afterall, in order to positively disrupt, vulnerability is a necessary pre-requisite.

Holding All at Once

An additional challenge of working through a transformational leadership lens is being able to hold space for everything and everyone at once. I see this as perhaps the most difficult challenge because it requires a level of generosity and use of self that is very much connected to a higher order purpose. I have met people in my work who are able to hold space for many identities and experiences all at once. They refer to themselves as Global Citizens. These are usually those individuals from multiracial and multicultural backgrounds who have had to negotiate many different spaces and share feeling a part of and separate from all of these spaces all at once. They reach beyond their ways of knowing and being and figuratively enter into the lives of others while suspending judgment and holding on tight to compassion. I am not sure if this is a skill to be taught or if it is both a skill and something that comes innate to those of us who have spent our life moving between and within different and diverse spaces, while also knowing that true inclusion is not possible in the context of the binary and exclusive ideology that grounds this country.

If we do try to foster the ability to hold all at once, this is where the trait and tool of being comfortable with nuance comes into play. Traditional social work and leadership training did not prepare us to hold the experiences of white and Black and Brown folks all at once. Traditional training also did not prepare us for the intersections of trauma-informed practice and diversity and inclusion. While, the siloed approach is much more common, it leads to exclusive spaces that do not build community or foster growth and hold up the status quo. Traditional organizational cultures as well as schools of social work and higher education are traditionally siloed, each person operating in their "expert" comfort zones. Yet, the cross pollination of practice and expertise innately builds diversity, community and pushes back against white supremacy. Yet the irony is that social workers should be equipped to do just that, hold all at once.

We discussed in an earlier chapter how organizations are either driven toward a trauma-informed mission or a diversity, equity and inclusion mission. This project hopes to provide us with the tools to create a truly inclusive organizational culture that is able to live in both spaces simultaneously. The act of holding all at once means being able to see the nuance in difference and having the skills to attend to the diversity and inclusion and trauma in any space.

When I think of the intersections of trauma and diversity and inclusion, I think of the classroom and the different experiences of students of color and white students. Recently, a few of my colleagues have been vulnerable about sharing their challenges with holding space for white students and Black, Indigenous and students of color, especially in classroom discussions of the COVID-19 pandemic. I had a white and male colleague reach out to me after Ahmaud Arbery was murdered. He was finishing up his last class of the semester and right before he ended the class, a Black female student started to cry and talk openly about how this tragedy and the impact of COVID-19 on the Black and African American community, in general, was affecting her. While other students of color validated her feelings and offered their own and similar perspectives, the majority of the white students remained quiet. It was the last class of the semester and so my colleague was concerned about ending in this way. He also wanted to discuss ways to engage the white students who remained quiet. I have witnessed this quite a bit, white students staying quiet during discussions on race because "they do not know what to say." Or similar to the executive, "they do not want to say the wrong thing." In these moments, silence becomes a privilege. That is, the privilege to opt out of the conversation and remain quiet. I suggested to my colleague that he sends an individual email to each student asking the student what was going on for them internally when this discussion was taking place? I suggested that he be explicit in his email for those students who remained quiet. I suggested that he voice his observation in an email by writing something along the lines of how he noticed that they were quiet. I encouraged him to honor curiosity and ask what was going on for them in that moment. I also suggested that he model vulnerability and share how he felt as a white and male instructor in that moment, trying to navigate a diverse classroom in a space of racial trauma. Holding space for the trauma of racism coupled with the guilt and shame experienced by white students is a tall order. We also spoke about the acceptance that such conversations do not always have a "closure." That is, part of the challenge in social justice work is accepting non-closure and being okay with unfinished conversations. Yet, if we return to the classroom setting for a moment, there was an opportunity here for positive disruption that did not occur. There was the possibility and potential to exist in a truly inclusive space where all bodies could have engaged with racial trauma from their diverse vantage points. The instructor could have used the skills of mindfulness, curiosity, compassion, nuance, empathic accountability, trauma responsiveness and vulnerability to hold the collective trauma, within a space of diversity and inclusion. All bodies in their various identities could have collaboratively engaged in a brave dialogue where they unpacked their individual responses collectively, including silence. Especially for the instructor, the practice of holding all at once is challenging in its use of self, ambiguity and uncertainty. At the same time, the potential and possibility for understanding diversity, fostering inclusion and ultimately collective healing, is huge. Instead, what did end up happening was the space was created for a healthy conversation for only some of the bodies in the room, while others were allowed to opt out only to have their concerns aired privately after the fact with someone who racially identifies in the same way. We see here how the personal work intersects with the professional work. The personal work is use of self in the classroom where identity is always relevant.

When considering issues, skills and concerns around holding all at once, I am again reminded of the current COVID-19 pandemic and the need to address the trauma and grief of all lives lost while also holding and engaging with the disparate impact on the Black, Indigenous and people of color and their communities. I am reminded of the Black Lives Matter movement and the All Lives Matter appeal for those who don't know, simply don't care, and hold explicitly racist attitudes toward Black lives. All Lives Matter disregards and attempts to invalidate the systemic racism and precarity that surrounds Black Lives in the United States. Representing Black Lives Matter does not cancel out all other Lives, it is a reminder and explicit call out that Black bodies currently and historically have not been valued as much as white bodies, and there are infinite examples that speak to this. I am reminded of the anti-semitic and anti-racism hierarchy of oppression debate. Upholding a commitment to anti-racism does not cancel out or lessen the pain of anti-semitism. The dichotomous either-or thinking invites silos instead of nuance and complexity. Somehow, the elevation of the experiences of Black and Brown people becomes threat to systems. The coupling of the trauma between my parents, with the trauma of naming myself in spaces where my identities were divorced, created the conditions that lead me to approach this work from the lens of inclusion and generosity. For me, holding empathically accountable spaces for all was and is a survival mechanism but for many I do realize how challenging it is.

Well Intentioned Ideology of Social Work

The well-intentioned ideology of the social work profession impedes our ability to look deeply at issues of race, class and gender, and specific to this project, the ways that structural racism impacts leadership. In my classrooms and my workshops, I speak a lot about the difference between intention vs. impact. The well-intentioned ideology of social work is guarded by a good intention mind frame. Meaning, as long as your intentions are good and you are kind, that is all that matters. After all, social work is a helping profession that is proliferated with kind people who want to do good. However, without locating yourself in your purpose of social work, there is the possibility that your privilege can shield you from understanding the impact of your actions on others. While your intention may be to help, the impact may show up as being patronizing or paternalistic, especially when working with marginalized clients and communities. Are you considering your social location and the impact of your identity, actions and words on others, even in the space of good intention? Good intention alone also stops us from doing the deep personal work of racial accountability that is required of in this type of leadership. Good intention also shields us from the hurt we may have caused others by not considering ourselves and the impact of our power and privilege.

An additional issue that arises is when social workers work in communities, which they are not familiar with. The skills and literature taught on cultural competency provide the social worker with an achieved status or competence as it relates to culture that falls short of reality. Cultural competency is a soft ask for social workers that does not include self-interrogation in the form of locating yourself in the work. Cultural competency does not include an analysis of white organizational culture. It is much easier to be guided by an ideology of good intention than it is to do the work of locating ourselves in that intention and assessing the impact, but as long as this phrase remains without being reworked, then opportunities for positive disruption will be thwarted.

Rather than just considering good intention, we must also assess what impact said intention yields. Without assessing the impact there is the potential for exclusion of other ways of knowing and from the receiver. Meaning, while we may not always know what our impact was on the receiver, we can honor the skills of courage, vulnerability and curiosity and ask. Meaning arises through dialogue. Assuming that the receiver understood our good intention and that it landed positively means that we are operating from an objective reality. We are operating only from our way of knowing. Without checking out the impact, leaves the act open for interpretation and possibly exclusion from the receiver. This is challenging because it requires an intentionality and way of being that are more nuanced and more mindful than before. It certainly deepens the relationship between the actors while also adding an additional layer of work.

Time

Transformational leadership takes time and investment in yourself. How do we actually make this work a priority in an already over stressed system or in systems that value quantity over quality? In systems where process is also not seen as the product. I first think of the supervisory process in social work. Supervision, in many organizations is seen as a luxury. I learned from my own experience and from speaking with others, that it is usually the first thing to go when there is time-sensitive pressure on other tasks. Yet, it is perhaps the most valuable resource for support, education and potentially for personal growth. This parallels the prior discussion of COVID-19 and diversity, equity and inclusion being the first to go. When things are under pressure, devoting an hour to supervision might increase efficiency and quality on said tasks. It is also the place where social workers can assess their ongoing commitment to social justice in their role as leaders in the organization. In a field that works with and for people, there is a great need for task and clinical supervision.

Next, I think of the culture of organizations. In an organizational setting, individual coaching sessions are keys to building relationships with leaders to help them shift to a transformational mindset, yet these sessions are also time consuming. The personal work involved in locating yourself in your role as a leader and the impact on the organizational culture takes both time and resources. The demands on time are a reality. One-off training is an easy solution to introducing diversity, equity and inclusion, and certainly a time saver, but then what happens after that training? How is the learning and challenges involved in that work integrated and sustained in the organization? Furthermore, what happens when you run into challenges along the way? Or are faced with those moments in meetings when you do not know what to say or how to enter a conversation? Coaching provides leaders with the relationship to be vulnerable and to continually process the journey.

Value to the Organization and to Social Work Practice

This brings us to the challenge of values. What value does trauma-informed diversity and inclusion work have to the organization? What value does it have in social work practice? Will this lens and subsequent work live at the top of the list when there are other competing factors? This work meaning, not the one-off diversity and implicit bias trainings, but the heart felt work of transformational leadership as defined and described in this project. Combating workplace bias in the form of a diversity training is much different than investing in transformational leading. I have noticed in my consulting and in my work at the University that once the COVID-19 pandemic hit, diversity, equity and inclusion became siloed, it was not a felt need and so the "work" was no longer a priority. As a stark example, social justice was never given the same priority as the transition to online learning. Creating inclusive, diverse and equitable spaces was not given the same worth in organizations as fundraising and marketing. This begged the question of, *what do leaders in higher education and in organizations place value on, especially in a crisis.* In one non-profit organization I work with the diversity, equity and inclusion committee was "put on a hold," until the organization "returned to normalcy." Yet for this particular organization the "return to normalcy" goal was interrupted by the resurgence of the Black Lives Matter movement. What an organization spends time messaging about, funding and securing resources for often gives me a clue as to what the organization places value on.

In addition, when brought on to facilitate workshops and groups I am always asked what my consulting fee is. One of my first questions back to my client is what funds do you have set aside to do this work? Not only do I want to be mindful about working within a budget, especially for non-profits, this figure often gives me insight into what value the organization places on diversity and inclusion. This also becomes a conversation before the actual work even starts. I would be remiss not to question the value that is placed on the benefits of this lens and practice model. How much value is placed on shifting the lens away from traditional forms of leadership to a framework that is truly grounded in social justice and humanity? With that comes a cost.

Ego and Status

Ego and perceived and internalized status are a challenge. Leaders get comfortable in their roles. The psychology of the leader is a factor and potentially a challenge in shifting to this lens. On some level, immersion in this lens of leadership means equalizing relationships where the traditional "all knowing" leader instead works in collaboration with others. How much does a leader gain from the perceived status of being a leader? How much of a leader's identity is tied to the success of any company? The binary constructions of right and wrong, with the pressure of leaders to always be right is a challenge when thinking of adopting an approach to leadership that requires an internal look at the psychology behind what someone gains from a leadership position. I have compassion for leaders who feel they have the weight of the organization on their shoulders, especially during a crisis. Fear and anxiety are very real emotions that can manifest in ways that limit the potential to lean into colleagues. Labels such as "boss" and "chief" denote a higher being status that can be very connected to self-worth and identity. Even the notion of mastery brings with it a pressure that may block self-compassion. This has the potential to corrupt relationships, decrease creativity and productivity, and lessen the potential for inclusive spaces.

Reflection

There are challenges to working from a transformational leadership lens. Often times there is a catalyst that pushes us to challenge the discourse and sometimes there is regression or relapse but with that also comes an awareness to what triggers us to pause or re-set the journey toward sincere inclusion.

Discussion Questions

1. Review the list of white organizational culture traits. Where do you see any of these traits show up for you?
2. Which challenges resonated with you?
3. How do we notice and seize opportunities of positive disruption?
4. In what ways are you able to take more risks?
5. Are we able to see these as moments of personal and professional growth? While also recognizing that disruption may also cause trauma.

References

Okun, T. (n.d.). *Dismantaling racism.* Retrieved from http://www.dismantlingracism.org/white-supremacy-culture.html

Okun, T., & Jones, K. (2001). *White supremacy organizational culture.* Retrieved from Dismantling Racism. Available at https://www.dismantlingracism.org/uploads/4/3/5/7/43579015/okun_-_white_sup_culture.pdf

Kendi, I. X. (2019). *How to be an anti-racist.* New York, NY: Penguin Random House.

6

ENVISION A NEW

We are in a moment in 2020 with COVID-19 and the resurgence of the Black Lives Matter movement that I hope will turn into a sincere and sustained movement. This project is an effort toward helping the social work profession and the leadership space do just that. That is, create a social work field of practice, curricula within schools of social work, leadership style, organizational culture and classroom that is truly inclusive, trauma-informed and driven toward racial equity in every space. I imagine what it would have been like for me to be educated in all of my social work courses from a critical race lens where the reverence was not only for white scholars but also for scholars of Black, Indigenous and people of color backgrounds. Where more instructors looked like me or at the very least taught with a lens of trauma-informed diversity and inclusion. Where the textbooks and articles were written by BIPOC and the classroom spaces were brave forums of inclusion and diversity. So much of my formative years were spent on trying to fit into spaces that were not inclusive and questioning myself and my lived experience. I think of all the students and professors who occupy similar spaces as I did and of those students and professors who do not have an awareness of the critical need for diversity and inclusion. I yearn for liberatory classrooms and organizational cultures that are trauma-informed, inclusive and diverse. That means these cultures and classrooms are grounded in transparency and empathic accountability. I am reminded of Dr. Barbara Love's practice of developing a liberatory consciousness, where there exists the possibility to transcend current social constructions that limit the mind and heart from expanding beyond our socialization (Love, 2013). I am reminded of Audre Lorde's no hierarchy of oppression ideology and practice where identities are held and nurtured and united in peace. I am reminded of the shared goal of revolutionary love and liberation, particularly in this moment of COIVD-19 and the resurgence of the Black Lives Matter movement. I would argue that the field of social work has a responsibility in this moment to help guide the way. We are a field that innately engages the hearts and minds, that invests in personal and professional growth and that at its best, positively disrupts normative white culture to create space for marginalized bodies, voices and communities. I think back to my desire to obtain and PhD in Social Welfare. That desire was driven by a need to use my narrative and clinical experience in the field of trauma to teach social workers how to use themselves to, what I have now termed, positively disrupt the status quo. It is not a coincidence that my doctoral advisees are comprised of those students, primarily students of color, who desire to fill a gap in the literature by using their own narratives combined with their social work professional experiences in leadership roles to also positively disrupt. The social work person-in-environment framework begs for an explicit integration of micro, meso and macro practice and for continuous and sincere dialogues about race, racism and whiteness in every space. I would further argue that social work leaders in the field and in the academy have an additional responsibility to learn how to model and even lead these dialogues, creating brave spaces for staff, faculty, supervisees and students to engage in critical discussions centered on white supremacy culture, trauma, diversity and inclusion that permeate every aspect of an organization, a curriculum and a supervisory session. Can we envision a new for the social work profession where the traits, tools and practice principles become the norm in how social workers and leaders in the field engage with one another and with staff, students and clients? I am reminded of one specific example of attending a faculty meeting when I raised the question of the desire to hold ourselves and our community accountable, in an effort to sincerely serve the diversity of students we work with. That request was not met with open arms, I am wondering if in this moment the felt defensives surrounding discussions of accountability has shifted?

In this moment of reflection; take a minute to locate yourself in this project. What resonates for you? What do you feel particularly challenged by? Now that we have identified the challenges, how do we begin to imagine the integration of a transformational lens to leadership?

This chapter is called Envision a New because that is exactly what I would like for you to do. Envisioning a New does not necessarily mean throwing out the old. It means an integration of the traits and tools identified in the previous chapters to envision a new work culture, a new classroom, a new meeting space or interaction where sincere inclusion exists. Mindfulness, compassion, comfortability with nuance, courage, vulnerability, empathic accountability, curiosity and being trauma responsive are the tools and traits that ground positive disruption and guide a way of being and a leadership that is trauma-informed and diverse and inclusive.

I have found in my work at the university and with the organizations I work with that the hardest part of trauma-informed leadership from the lens of diversity and inclusion is the integration and sustainability of it. Once the contract, class or dialogue ends, how is the work both integrated into the larger system and sustained? Once the act of police brutality and outrage disappears from the news and the social media posts move onto something else, how is this work sustained? Because this approach is an ideology and not just a checklist, it requires a shift in mindset. Sustaining that mindset and practice takes a culture of empathic accountability, support, intentionality, time and commitment.

Social Justice and Disruption

The theory and practice of positive disruption is central to incorporating diversity and inclusion into trauma-informed leadership. It is this mindset and act that fosters social justice. Social work is grounded in a social justice mandate. If you think about it, positive disruption is an operationalization of that mandate. Essentially, the goal of disruption is to give voice and space to experiences that have been left out of the conversation, or that feel unwelcomed. The lens of diversity and inclusion, and subsequent interpersonal and systemic racial trauma, has been left out of trauma-informed practice and leadership. Yet, we must start with locating ourselves to first identify where we live in these spaces, what implicit biases we may be harboring, what emotional baggage are we carrying and what fears are stunting our growth and sincere engagement with the social justice mission of social work.

Let's revisit where we started.

Locating Self

Locate yourself. Revisit your purpose for pursuing a Masters in Social Work. Why did you choose social work? Think deeply about your socialization process, the messages you received growing up, the communities you live in today, the company you keep, the books you read and the music you listen to. Think about your work with clients and communities who are different then you in race, culture, religion, gender, sexual orientation and class. Where does your discomfort lie?

Positive Disruption

Next, think about the theory and practice of positive disruption. Disruption may feel uncomfortable and unsettling. It is a rupture to the system characterized by uncertainty, ambiguity and disturbance, and it is making room for more, more nuance, more complexity, more inclusion. Do you feel any different about disruption now compared to when we first started? Since beginning this project, have you found yourself in any situations that warrant disruption, and have you handled these situations any differently than you may have prior? Take a few minutes to reflect on and answer this question.

The How, Why, When of Positive Disruption

The ways that we disrupt are as important as why and when we disrupt. I use the adjective positive before disruption intentionally. As discussed earlier, negative disruption is when the dialogue turns into a debate, when divisions within communities of color are centered instead of unity, or when people who were on the right path and went wrong somewhere along the way are criticized heavily rather than taught and shown their error, when hierarchy of oppression debates dominates the conversation. Social workers are taught "use of self" early in their education, but social workers are not taught how to use ourselves sincerely or strategically to disrupt systems of oppression, despite our social justice mandate. Social workers are taught skills of advocacy and empowerment but not positive disruption. Effective positive disruption first involves the internal work. That is, the process of locating yourself as you have been doing throughout this project. This is the step that is most often sidelined and the step that is most important in becoming effective in any disruption. The hardest and most crucial part of social justice work is the internal reflection before moving to external action. It is far easier to engage in external activities such as social media posting, signing petitions, donating and intellectualizing the injustice, then it is too look inward at our biases, privileges and, perhaps the most difficult, becoming aware of how we may have been benefitting and contributing to systemic oppression. What comes up for you when you think about the needed internal work? Are there ways in which you feel you have benefited or unknowingly contributed to systemic oppression? Take a few minutes to reflect on and answer these questions.

A very common example of contributing to systemic oppression is the act of staying silent about the realities of race and opting out of discussions because of felt discomfort talking about race and racial traumas. Social workers struggle with conversations about race and particularly about whiteness. White people are, for the most part, racially comfortable in the way spaces and institutions are constructed currently. Therefore, moving out of that space feels uncomfortable. An unearned advantage of being white is that for the most part, you are always surrounded by people and leaders who look like you. In the social work field, the people who do not look like you are usually not in positions of power. They are the clients and communities' social workers work with and work for. If there is not a level of engagement around race and an openness to talking about systemic racism and oppression, the work with the clients and communities of color is inherently insincere. The reality and lived experience of living while Black is denied. Once we take the time to do the internal work, the mindfulness slowly shifts and we may become more intentional about asking ourselves what is the best way to disrupt for the specific circumstance? In other words, how will we be most effective in our delivery? On some level, this means accepting the limits of our power and influence. Meaning, I can speak from my heart and even present evidence of injustice, but I cannot expect that my words or actions will change a person or a system. In going about positive disruption, your focus should be maximizing your ability and effectiveness in opening up a person or system to a different perspective. Being forcefully right is not effective if it "falls on deaf ears." As discussed earlier, I strive to "enter" without any expectation of anything more than awareness. This way my training, dialogue, discussion or conversation does not turn into a debate or a convincing, but rather a sharing of vulnerability and compassion for the pain and the shame of others. While doing this, I simultaneously create a community of empathic accountability and support to lean into. I cannot do this work alone. Because the emotionality involved is intense and the giving of myself is physically, psychologically and spiritually exhausting, I need a community to hold me accountable during the times I am not operating from a sincere and generous space.

Locating Myself

I have become increasingly intentional about how I use myself as an instructor, an educator and as a facilitator in organizational spaces and in the University. Finally, during the COVID-19 pandemic and the concurrent protests, police brutality and racial trauma, I have been asked to provide more individual coaching to executives, CEOs and leaders in the Human Resource space. I have also been asked to speak in larger forums on the intersections of trauma, social justice and compassion. In those platforms, which are now all via video conferencing due to the COVID-19 pandemic, I am very much aware of the limitation of being able to literally and physically reach many people. The online platform is fraught with compassion fatigue and an inability to sit face to face with someone or a group of people and feel their struggle. There is never enough time. I can't feel their energy or notice non-verbal communication when I am sharing a screen. The audience is usually between 40 and 180 people depending on the organization. My audience during these talks are CEOs, executive staff and social workers, supervisors, managers and direct service providers. I am aware of the privilege of being able to opt out and how the ability to opt out discreetly is so much easier on Zoom and in virtual sessions in general. The modes in which one may opt out is even expanded on said platforms, as the audience has the ability to disengage, stay silent or even shut off their video completely. To counter this, I explicitly state just that, that there is more of an option during a zoom or virtual session to opt out of a difficult conversation, but if we are going to do the work of social justice, it requires being uncomfortable. I ask participants to turn on their cameras and ask if I may call on them in moments of silence. I also explicitly state that the chat box is to ask questions but not to engage in continued dialogue.

Typically, I have somewhere between 30 minutes to an hour and a half to speak about grief, loss, disparity, social work supervision, the disparate impact on the Black community, all coupled with the police brutality and protesting we are witnessing and taking part in. I ground myself in compassion and my goal in these talks is to be able to hold space for everyone. I am intentional and mindful about explicitly touching on each topic from a place of vulnerability. I am constantly using myself to help the audience connect and locate themselves as I too, am locating myself in the moment. I state this explicitly. I do my best to structure the talk as I would a workshop in physical space, by starting with an introduction as to why I do this work and ground us in the current moment. I then review a guide for community engagements. I use the screen as I would my body if I were in a face-to-face setting. Meaning, moving back and forth between sharing a screen of a power point to closing it out to pause, reflect and open up the mics, and monitor and respond to the chat box, even in very large groups. I directly state that it is hard to get a pulse of the room from a virtual space and so if I could have folks pose questions in the chat or share verbally that would help me gauge where folks are at and what resonated for them in all I have said thus far. My intention is not only to get my message across but to engage the audience, build community and move them to a deeper place.

Of special interest during these times are issues of systemic racism and police brutality. While these have always been concerns in communities of color, its focus in media, national discourse and accompanying public outcry has created interest in diversity and inclusion work in the corporate and non-profit sector. I do not only want to create the space for Black participants to express the outrage of police brutality and racial trauma, I also want to help white folks in the audience tap into their feelings of helplessness, shame and fears of stepping up. I have facilitated dialogues where white folks start off by being vulnerable and sharing, allowing the BIPOC in the room a moment to rest, breathe and choose to share or not share. I have also facilitated dialogues where BIPOC begin by sharing their pain and exhaustion. Their testimonials are left often with a felt silence, which I acknowledge, and then invite white folks into the space to share what they heard, and how they heard it. From a place of curiosity and compassion, I engage them in a discussion on how they have been complicit in systemic racism and the racial trauma of Black, Indigenous, people of color.

I want to hold the grief and loss that is universal, while also emphasizing racial trauma, the impact on the Black community and structural racism. The theme that resonates for me in every space I enter, is the use of self as the tool for transformation. Using the traits and tools of mindfulness, curiosity, compassion, vulnerability, nuance, trauma responsiveness and courage to lead and create a trauma-informed culture that is grounded in a diversity and inclusion lens.

Discussion Questions

1. What does envisioning a new look like for you, personally and professionally?
2. What does envisioning a new specifically in social work look like? Be creative here, feel free to write or draw.
3. Where do you see opportunities for improvement?
4. Where have you felt excluded from the dialogue? Where have you unintentionally excluded others?
5. As a leader in an organization, what does envisioning a new look like for you?
6. Where do you see opportunities for improvement?
7. As a social work supervisor, what does envisioning a new look like in your supervision? What improvements can you make? Where can you be braver, more compassionate, more curious?

References

Love, B. (2013). Developing a liberatory consciousness. In W. B. M. Adams (Ed.), *Readings for diversity and social justice* (pp. 601–605). New York, NY: Routledge.

Lorde, A. (1983). There is no hierarchy of oppression. *Bulletin: Homophobia and Education*, (3/4), 9, 14.

TRAININGS, WORKSHOPS AND DIALOGUES

Through a Trauma-Informed, Diversity and Inclusion Lens

I would like to share with you more concrete ways that I teach, train and facilitate through a trauma-informed diversity and inclusion lens. What is crucial to consider when reading the next part of this chapter, is how you are using yourself and integrating the traits and tools of trauma-informed leadership from the lens of diversity and inclusion. As a reminder, these traits and tools are; mindfulness, compassion, comfortability with nuance, courage, vulnerability, empathic accountability, curiosity and being trauma responsive.

The facilitation of groups, trainings, workshops and dialogues is crucial to the success of any program. Some initial questions I have for potential facilitators include; How much are you willing to be vulnerable? How much are you able to take your time moving through the material at a pace that is both efficient and also nurturing to what comes up? Are you able to sit in moments of silence and let folks wrestle with the material until someone in the group speaks first before you? This space cannot be a forum for you to expose your ideas, ideologies, or ways of being. This is not a space for goal-oriented progress with an end date and certificate of accomplishment.

It is a forum to engage in vulnerability and share as a point of reference and as a way to help participants unpack and share.

As mentioned, the specific ways in which you use yourself as the facilitator is essential to the outcome. Facilitation is an art. For example, moving back and forth between process and content, and paying attention to implicit and explicit content in the space. Meaning, listening deeply to what people are saying, suspending judgement and paying close attention to affect, tone and nuance of how and what participants are saying. As the facilitator this means that you cannot approach sessions with a concrete planned discussion. You may know an intended point of departure, but you should be guided by the flow of organic conversation. When conversation is not productive or stalling, you can push it in certain directions explicitly or implicitly via nudging. For example, when there is silence, I often ask about the silence. I reframe my question, or I open up the space for people to share what they are experiencing in this moment that is causing the silence. This organic use of self presents a challenge for some facilitators who desire a road map or a step by step guide. I have co-facilitated sessions with some facilitators who spend the majority of the time looking at the guide or curriculum instead of focusing on the energy in the space. These facilitators have shared that the use of self feels ambiguous and scary, reading from a "script" feels easier. They do recognize that the result is that by staying focused just on the material, they miss out on crucial nuances and opportunities to go deeper, beyond what is being presented. Students have the opportunity to practice facilitation skills in the classroom through individual or group presentations. Presentations are a way to practice public speaking and use of self. Think about this as the difference between reading straight from a power point, or presenting the power point as a backdrop to your conversation or dialogue with the class. How can you, as students, take risks and use yourself more effectively in the classroom during these moments, engaging your classmates as you would your clients.

There are the formal trainings and workshops and then there are the forums and the dialogues. These practices are further explained below. Forums and dialogues serve as the starting and guiding point for a lifelong commitment to trauma-informed leadership and practice from the lens of diversity and inclusion.

Your role as a facilitator in more formal trainings, workshops and in dialogues is to make connections, pull out themes, challenge, validate and help move the dialogue along to a place of healing rather than a place of convincing. It is a space to develop shared meaning. For guidance, I look to the teachings of bell hooks (hooks, 1994) and my colleague and friend Dr. Rani Varghese and her work with a practice known as Intergroup Dialogue (Hunang-Nissen, 1999). Both require a deeper, more engaged, intentional and mindful use of self. We have all been in trainings where the facilitator talks, and talks, and talks, without an awareness as to the energy of the room. The ways in which you begin any workshop, training or dialogue is important in setting the tone and helping participants re-enter their worlds after they leave the space you created for that allotted time period, knowing that this is the beginning of relationship building and will continue over time.

Workshop and Training from a Trauma-informed, Diversity and Inclusion Lens

Intersections of Trauma, Social Justice and Compassion

This is a workshop and training that is designed to help participants identify and use the intersections of trauma and diversity and inclusion in their practice. The ways in which I train are a parallel process to the work with clients and staff. I make that explicit. This training can be used in times of crisis, trauma or change. This workshop was used specifically during COVID-19 and the resurgence of the Black Lives Matter movement. The goal was to find a bridge to these experiences for the social work community. During this time, many social workers expressed a desire for a training solely focused on COVID-19. Given my trauma-informed and diversity and inclusion ideology and practice, I felt the need to help social workers find the intersectionality in this moment and further deepen their connection to the social justice mission of our profession. I recommend in any training or workshop for social workers that their lives, somewhere in the curriculum, an explicit connection to social justice. That way, the social justice mission does not become siloed but actually lives and thrives in all spaces. This explicit connection supports our envisioning a new framework within the field of social work.

1. Welcome: I start by thanking everyone for sharing space with me. Starting off with gratitude and also an acknowledgment that I do not know people and that they do not know me, and that always makes me a little nervous. Modeling vulnerability from the very start helps relax into the space. I ask everyone to bring or get, if they do not have one in the moment, a journal so they can take notes and record thoughts throughout the session. A general introduction about who I am and why I do this work. I begin with an intentional, mindful, collaborative and inclusive mindset. I lean into the commonality in the room. For example, in a training for social workers, I state social work and the mission of social justice as the common factor despite the diverse array of roles and positions participants may occupy. For organizations and executive meetings, I draw on the values of the organization to ground us in a common space.

    a. Recognize the grief and loss that is sitting with us as we navigate a time that is ambiguous, uncertain and filled with constant readjustment. Acknowledge the diversity and nuance in the room while centering inclusion.
    b. In a virtual space I uplift moments of increased intimacy: We are engaging from behind a screen. With that we lose the energy of being physically close and literally sharing space. In a virtual space, folks may also be experiencing compassion fatigue. Yet, because we are in the space of our homes, we are able to engage our whole self in ways that were not available to us before. For example, we see into the rooms that we are working. The painting on the wall, or the favorite coffee mug. We sometimes hear the sounds of dogs barking or children stomping, crying or laughing. I may share where my kids are in this moment as I struggle to find the balance in it all.
    c. Discuss community agreement; speak from the "I," listen, notice how and when you may move in and out of the

conversation, expect to have non closure. Here is where we begin to create safety, bravery and trustworthiness which are some of the tenets of trauma-informed practice.

2. Check in: Take a few minutes to check in with everybody: I start the check in with sharing my opportunity and challenge. Helping participants ground themselves in this present moment of hope and pain. In a face to face setting, I have a dry erase board that I use to document their opportunities and challenges. Sometimes I respond to a participant and sometimes I stay silent throughout the activity. This decision depends on what someone shares and if I can capitalize on it as a way to create additional awareness and build community. I present choice to the participants. I lean into vulnerability and curiosity. Empowering participants to speak their truth.

    a. Identify two opportunities that have also been a source of positive coping for you. One personally and one in your work. I reframe opportunity as a way to cope, sharing experiences of my own first as a way to model.
    b. Identify two challenges; personally, and in your work.

3. Locate myself: I locate myself as an Associate Professor, single mom and woman of color. These are the complexities of my identity that hold both privilege and oppression. Sharing my story models compassion, courage, vulnerability and allows the participants to hold me accountable. This is always an interesting moment because sharing yourself in a training or class is not a normative activity. Here we are using a narrative approach and vulnerability to build connection and emotional safety.

    a. Why is this relevant? I enter this space in all of my identities and ways of knowing.
    b. Acknowledge my privilege and platform: As a professor I have privilege and a platform. As a woman of color with a white mother I have also benefited from light skin privilege. Speaks to the nuance and need for compassion.

c. Strive for gratitude: I do my best each and every day to exist in a place of gratitude.
d. Embrace the messiness: The work of social justice is messy, uncomfortable and personal.
e. Past triggers resurfacing: We are in a moment of complex trauma and it is normal that past traumas resurface as we are triggered. This is an explicit integration of trauma and a modeling of the need for self-compassion and compassion for others.
f. Acceptance/Presence: A radical acceptance of where we are in every moment is necessary, even when it feels hard and uncomfortable.

Present this question to the audience. Depending on the size of the group, I may pair participants up for 10 minutes and then have a report back from each group. Or do this exercise as a group and ask for volunteers to share.

4. Acknowledge the collective vulnerability we are all experiencing, in very different ways.

   a. Offer concrete examples of disparity and inequity. For example, that shelter-in place is a privilege. The impact of wearing a mask and how it shows up differently for Black men. This is another explicit integration of trauma and social justice.

5. Mindfulness of self and other.

   a. Opportunity here and now to engage in the practice of mindfulness. I talk about the intentionality of language and the practice of mindfulness to notice privilege and bias. I engage the practice of mindfulness to help white folks engage in self compassion in order to work through hand move past the shame and fragility of whiteness. I question the whole group, what has stopped us from considering others?

6. How are we examining our own personal positionalities and experiences, along with critically examining the pandemic's

disparate impact on families and local communities? Directly related to person-in-environment.

a. Widening the lens and adopting a trauma-informed ideology of inclusion that positively disrupts spaces that exclude the most vulnerable. For BIPOC, this is an additional layer.

This question calls for a small group exercise, or break out groups in an online setting. Have participants work in small groups for 15 minutes and the report back to the larger group. As a facilitator, you are capitalizing on the themes, practicing curiosity, compassion, being trauma responsive, vulnerable and maintaining the courage to probe responses when necessary and unpack rhetoric.

7. Next, we move into action steps, how can we do better? This can range in scope. The idea is to hold the process and action in the same space, while acknowledging that everyone is in a different place. It is important in this moment to encourage participants to find those quiet spaces of personal accountability. Encourage participants to lean into the discomfort while also finding your resilience. Being mindful of the time throughout the session and reminding participants how much time they have left is important.
8. At about five minutes remaining I move into closure. Reminding participants that we must accept non closure due to the nature of the topic. I share the difficulty with that and encourage participants to continue thinking, processing and even keeping a journal to record their journey in this work. I end with asking participants to say one adjective or a few words on how they are leaving the space and if they have thought of any ways to employ these practices in their personal lives.

Open Forum Format: One to One-And-A-Half-Hour Time Slot

Recently, because of the racial trauma that has erupted and the desire for organizations to create space for a shift in culture. I have been asked to hold space for the members of various organizations. This type of forum is best in moments of change. Change as a society and change in organizations. It is also used in times of crisis and/or when diversity, equity and inclusion work is beginning in an organization or classroom. The goal being to build community and gather as a collective opening up people and the systems to different perspectives, beginning with the sharing of space and voice. I have used this space as an information gathering tool to begin to unpack where the organization sits in the diversity, equity and inclusion space. While also, engaging staff in the personal work that is needed. When organizations decide to hire me, an email is sent out to the company introducing me and identifying an hour that the organization will meet as a whole. In this present moment of trauma, employees enter this forum with many diverse experiences. I am holding white guilt often expressed in the form of tears, Black and Brown anger, pain and a general feeling of helplessness among all staff and leadership. For organizations that never have done any diversity, equity and inclusion work before these forums become *the* place where past and present racial trauma is shared. Many staff have lived in a place of denial of racism and the ways they were complicit in upholding the status quo.

Forum and Dialogue Format

Trauma-informed Diversity and Inclusion is the framework and approach to this forum and dialogue. As the facilitator you are acknowledging that participants may share their traumas, you offer the opportunity to share from many diverse vantage points and lived experiences and remain inclusive of all of it.

The forum is designed in an open forum format. This space is very different from a training or workshop. The goal is to have participants show up and share where they are at in the moment. This differs from a workshop or training where the goal is to actively and explicitly teach or train. This is a facilitated discussion and my role is the facilitator as opposed to a trainer. My goals again are to guide the discussion and share with participants, not to convince or train. This should be made explicit to the participants.

It is my hope that participants approach the dialogue form a place of compassion and curiosity. Meaning, if I or members share and there is confusion around meaning then participants honor curiosity and ask questions rather than make assumptions. Often times assumptions are made and as the facilitator that should be attended to immediately. In a virtual space, the chat box is often used as an alternative to verbal dialogue which can be distracting to the material. As a facilitator in a virtual space the chat box is another area of attending to. As previously mentioned, private and public chats can take place during the training and may undermine or distract from what is being said and people may end up having conversations among themselves instead of with the whole group.

I also realize that the forum and dialogue format is different from traditional organizational culture. Personal dialogue in a work space and in a classroom is sometimes new and not normative. If participants are unable to listen to people share without judging or assuming, then it is a hard place to be in. It also is evident that deep listening, suspending judgement, asking questions and sharing is hard for some people in general and especially a work space and even in a classroom. Here is where the acute mindfulness and intentionality of the facilitator comes into practice.

The question surrounding whether or not personal dialogue in a workspace be mandatory is a leadership question. The benefits are that it builds community. You actually get to know your co-workers and hear their stories and their challenges including their traumas. There is a greater investment in human capital when stories are shared and the work place becomes a more intimate place of accountability and healing. When the organizational culture and classroom become a trauma-informed space of diversity and inclusion there is less emotional baggage for BIPOC because there is freedom to being able to bring your whole self to work and a feeling of being seen.

I encourage leaders and instructors to follow up with their staff and students following a forum. For the person who did not speak during the forum, I would explore with them why.

Here Is How I Hold These Forums

Introduction

I start with an introduction of who I am and why I do this work. I explicitly state that the hour allotted is not nearly enough time to express all the pain and shame that surfaced over the years and particularly in this present moment. I express that social justice work is a journey and similar to trauma work, unfolds over time, as the work becomes integrated into the organizational culture. I share my privileges in this space and some examples of organizations that have been successful in a sincere integration of diversity, equity and inclusion into their culture, how many years that took them and how we still face obstacles almost on the daily basis. I acknowledge that being Black in predominately white institutions is a trauma in and of itself, and that reality has stopped many Black people from bringing their wholes selves to work. Ultimately out goal is to create a compassionate, inclusive and accountable organizational culture that is grounded in our definition of trauma-informed leadership.

Community Engagements

These community engagements are crucial for creating a safe enough and brave space. I lean into the work of my social work, specifically group work, education and social justice mentors who came before me and helped me understand the importance of community engagements.

- A central community agreement is to intentionally and mindfully notice how you are engaging and listening today. When are the moments that you check out, shift in our seat, experience an emotional response? This is the mindfulness that is needed to identify where your internal work is. What exactly are you reacting to and where does it live in your body? What evokes emotion for you when I am speaking and when colleagues are speaking? Speak your truth to that in this space. If you do not speak your truth then think about why this is.

- Speak from the "I." In these conversations there is a tendency to generalize or use pronouns like "they" and "we." Own your words. Leaning into the trauma-informed tenet of empowerment.
- Finally for now, this conversation does not have closure. You may leave here feeling uncomfortable, with questions and/or with more to say. That is good. It means there is more work to do. Accept that this is a journey.

Hopes and Challenges: Pulling Themes

We then move into a more structured conversation about hopes and challenges. I remind folks to be conscious of the fact that there are many participants in this space and so we must move in and move out to be sure others have time to speak. In thinking about this present moment or attending this forum, what are your hopes and what do you feel challenged by? I give participants the choice of speaking from the heart if the questions feel too structured. I sometimes respond to the comments as they are shared, pulling themes, using my skills as a qualitative researcher and clinician, and leaning into vulnerability by sharing narratives from my work, with organizations, my students and my personal life. I become a story teller in these moments as I use myself to elicit vulnerability and open up a brave and transparent space. After about 20 minutes of this, I close the conversation with the acknowledgement that it never is actually closed.

Action Steps

We end with a summary of what transpired and action steps. The actions steps begin with the internal. Find those quiet moments of personal accountability. Lean into the discomfort. Where are you in this moment of our time together? What can you do to move the work of social justice forward in your homes, with your circles of friends, in your departments and in the organization as a whole? For example, buy a journal, talk with a few friends, check in on a colleague whom you heard speak today. These internal moments will lead to societal change you just have to start with locating yourself and doing the work at home. At the same time, do you continue to practice self-care? Are you building your resiliency and identifying your protective factors to keep this work going?

We close with an adjective or two on how participants are leaving the space.

References

hooks, b (1994). *Teaching to transgress.* New York, NY: Routledge.

Hunang-Nissen, S. (1999). *Dialogue groups: A practical guide to facilitate diversity conversation.* Blue Hill, NE: Medicine Bear Publishing.

CASE STUDIES

Next, we visit some case studies. I am grateful for the participants in these case studies all of whom occupy a diversity of identities and roles in social work and in for and non-profit organizations. I share these case studies as specific examples of the ways I have used myself to positive disrupt normative organizational culture through the relationships I have built with social work supervisors and leaders in organizations. Guided by the traits and tools of mindfulness, compassion, comfortability with nuance, courage, vulnerability, empathic accountability, curiosity and being trauma responsive, I have used trauma-informed social work practice and leadership from the lens of diversity and inclusion in my work with a diverse array of teams, leaders, supervisors and students. Below, you will read the intersections of my practice of trauma-informed leadership from a diversity and inclusion lens.

This first case study is an example that speaks to the construction of identity, the makers of identity and the impact of making assumptions as opposed to honoring curiosity. I see this case study as the intention for someone to disrupt and give voice to Black anger and pain while diminishing the complexity and nuance of race and racial identity. Let's revisit the discussion we had in the beginning of this project about the *multi-faceted ways in which inclusion could simultaneously be exclusionary, and the racialization that accompanies it.* I share this specific example, because it shows how important it is to first understand your connection to race before diving head first into this work. I am reminded of the work I have done on understanding and accepting the complexity of my identity and the trauma that accompanied that. The markers of identity I had to create which included an expansion of the socially constructed ones, especially when it came to what it means to be a woman of color, Latina, Biracial and Black.

This case study brings us back to the question of the traits and intentions involved in positive disruption. That is, mindfulness, compassion, comfortability with nuance, courage, vulnerability, empathic accountability, curiosity and being trauma responsive. Depending on our ways of knowing and stages of racial identity development, disruption can do more harm than good. In an attempt to include voice and experience, there is the potential to exclude others who may share similar experiences of racism and oppression but physically look different than us or identify different than us. For example, I have witnessed the internal struggle of Latinx social workers and staff with racial identity. How this group truly understands racial and cultural trauma but question their roles in the struggle for social justice because they have been told on more than one occasion that they are not Black. There is also the reality of anti-Black sentiment within the Latinx population and so by adopting a Black racial identity also requires a disruption in many families of origins. I have tackled some of these issues in my scholarship. My lived experience coupled with qualitative research helps readers better understand the impact of colorism within the Latinx population (Quiros & Araujo Dawson, 2013). In these moments I revisit the question of, are we in this to build a new, or create divides and tear people down?

Case Study: The Intersection of the Personal and the Professional: Negative Disruption When Woke Goes Wrong

I was facilitating a large forum for an organization I have been working with for about 2 years. An exercise start up organization. They brought me on because white leadership needed help with their whiteness and they sincerely wanted to create an inclusive and trauma-informed organization on every level. I worked with leadership, front desk, instructors and all the staff. My approach as it is with all of my clients, was open and accessible.

During one session, I left the forum early to attend another meeting. Staff was sharing when I said goodbye and they were in this moment of holding white leadership accountable. Shortly after, I get a text from the HR woman who I have been working closely with which read, *"they are saying you aren't Black." "They are questioning why we hired a consultant who isn't Black." "They are saying your website does not say you are Black."* Long story short, as soon as I left the forum, a biracial and Black identified staff member interrupted the sharing to question my assumed racial identity. After others chimed in, a Latinx woman who I had befriended while working there, spoke up in my absence. She explained my identity as she understood it, as a Latina, woman of color, also as Black. I ended up crafting a letter and sending it to the group.

I am writing and sharing with you, the reader, because of the complexity of this work that shows up in every space. I want to further emphasize the complexity which also lives in how people choose to identify and what those self-proclaimed makers of identity are. What does it mean to "not be Black enough?" What are the social constructions of Blackness and who gets to define that? Anti-Black sentiment is a real thing and the darker you are the more at risk you are for racial trauma. Can we hold that reality while also holding the reality that Blackness takes many forms and with that, the trauma of not being white is a constant reality for all BIPOC. One of the identified challenges in leading from a trauma-informed lens of diversity and inclusion is holding space for all. This country will never move forward if the dialogue of "Black enough" is not unpacked and stopped, and we shift focus to pushing back against white supremacy. I have spent the week collecting many many tears of white folks and sitting in and with Black and Brown rage, pain and anger. This experience is good because it is more for me to think about and directly address in my work and with clients and students. Even in an effort to shift and expand to create new understanding, the old dichotomies of either/or, Black or white, persist. What continues to get revealed is the inability to hold nuance, "both/and," or complexity. It is enraging and can be hurtful. It keeps us all in a two steps forward many steps back existence. I share this response letter with you. I could have let this sit and dissolve as most issues do over time but I model the accountability that I teach and so I felt a response was necessary.

Dear Community

Thank you for sharing space today. I understand there were some questions about my identity and I thought I would take this opportunity to address those directly. Let me begin by saying that as stated, I have been with the organization for 2 years. During those 2 years I have made myself vulnerable and my identity transparent. I have held space on several occasions, offered my email and phone number. Never once in 2 years has anyone asked me about any aspect of my identity whether it be How I identify? Or if they wonder, do I explicitly and directly benefit from the unearned advantages of my white mother? I welcome that dialogue and wonder why my identity was questioned after I left the call, or even at all?

My website says I identify as a woman of color. My mother is white and Jewish, and my dad Black and Latino. I have straddled the lines of anti-semitism and racism my whole life. Am I dark skinned? No. Do I identify as Black? Yes. Am I light skinned? Yes. Do I benefit from my mothers' white skin privilege? Yes. Have I experienced overt and implicit racism? Yes. Do I desire to be in liberatory spaces where I am not the only Latina or person of color? Yes.

You hired me because of my intersections of trauma and inclusion. Leadership hired me because I connected to the mission of inclusion and was also able to hold them accountable for unearned white privilege. I am not sure why the conversation shifted to my identity and I am really not sure how that is even relevant in this space. The Black experience is diverse and complex and filled with nuance and in some cases, light skinned privilege. What exactly does my assumed racial identity have to do with moving to a place of equity? And if that is still confusing, please, let's have that conversation from where I started and now, in the spirit of transparency.

I wonder how this country will move from a place of hurt, pain and shame to a place of healing. The human rights activist and author Arundhati Roy (2020) wrote that a crisis is a "portal, a gateway between one world and the next. We can choose to walk through it, dragging the carcasses of our prejudice and hatred, our avarice, our data banks and dead ideas, our dead rivers and smoky skies behind us. Or we can walk through lightly, with little luggage, ready to imagine another world. And ready to fight for it." Where are you?

I did receive some feedback after the letter was sent. The feedback came in the form of an apology for not having the dialogue when I was present and for an assumption of my identity. The staff was upset with white leadership's inaction and I was couched in that space. I leaned into my support network when this happened. It stung a little. My supports were there to check things out and process my reactions in order to move forward from a sincere place.

The next three case studies are also examples of my work. The first case study is from the perspective of a white and female client who I am currently coaching. She is the head of Human Resources from a technology start-up. The second case study is the voice of a former biracial and female doctoral student utilizing my practice of disruption in her place of work. The third case study is from the Head of Human Resources in a non-for-profit organization that I have been working with for a few years. An African American woman who I have befriended.

Case Study: White Cisgender Woman Head of Human Resources: When Professional Meets Personal

This case study is an example of how the work involved in professional positive disruption leads to disruption of personal spaces and community. We see this client disrupt the unnamed ideologies and spaces in both her personal and professional spaces. My work with her involved a close look at the organizational culture that was very much grounded in a white supremacy framework. Using resources such as Tema Okun's *White Supremacy Organizational Culture* (Okun & Jones, 2001) we looked closely at the ways the organization was operating and driven by a sense of urgency, perfectionism and fear of conflict. During our coaching sessions we talked about the intersection of her personal and professional spheres, her experiences growing up in her home and her college experience. All of which were formative in her white racial identity development. She lived and operated in spaces occupied primarily by white people and so, although considered herself a progressive woman, never really engaged in conversations about her whiteness or the unearned advantages of being white. She shared an experience of being pulled over by a police officer for speeding and shared her memory of the officer noticing her college bumper sticker on the back of her car. Instead of giving her a ticket, the conversation transitioned into talking about the liberal arts college she attended and the people they may have in common. The collaborative nature in which we worked together as well as some shared vulnerability from me, allowed us to move back and forth between her role in her organization and her personal trajectory. In all of these spaces she operated from a place of good intention coupled with the denial of her unearned privileges and the impact of living in a white dominated world. Following our second coaching session she shared that she was going to have a conversation with her white group of friends. Below is a recounting of my work with her and her organization.

> We started working with Dr. Laura Quiros in June 2020 as a company in order to be more inclusive, diverse, and understand how systemic racism is embedded in our work simply because of the deep roots of white supremacy in this country. It was important to us, as a company, to not do one training and be done, but rather make true systemic change with how the organization functions.
>
> I am the Head of People (HR, People Ops). At this time, I also started to do personal work and it quickly overlapped and was affected by the work we were doing with Dr. Laura Quiros as a company. She has helped me see how the personal work applies to company work, and back again.
>
> Some of the personal work has looked like this:
>
> 1. Read, watch, listen: social media, books, movies, music
> 2. Contribute: to organizations in Mississippi (where I live) that help the Black community
> 3. Start ancestral healing with an anti-racist focus
> 4. Have conversations with other White people

One of the most helpful actions has been conversations with White friends outside of work. We set these up to discuss White privilege and White supremacy with a group of all White friends.

Through working with Dr. Laura Quiros she has helped me much better understand my own Whiteness and how I contribute to systemic racism. In the conversations with White friends I was able to bring some of these learnings into the conversation.

Several themes came out of the conversations with White friends that gave me really fantastic insight into what some of my White colleagues might also be experiencing.

1. This is the first time some people are thinking about this at all.
2. People do not know what to do but they want to do something.
3. People are overwhelmed and sometimes paralyzed by the amount of materials being shared and are caught between very strong opinions of what is "right" and "wrong" way to approach this.

After reviewing this with Dr. Laura Quiros, she asked me if the personal work of talking to my white friends impacted my role in my organization in any way, which pushed me to think.

While this is only a sample of White people, having this conversation gave me at least some insight into what our majority White staff might be experiencing.

It was likely that this is the first time that many of our White team members at work were thinking about these topics. As leaders within the organization we can model how this work can look for White people.

So many of my White friends expressed a deep desire of what to do but not knowing what to do and feeling paralyzed by the amount of resources and possible actions. As an organization, simply telling White people what to do seemed like a helpful first step. If we as an organization can provide them with a direction to aim their energies, we are helping them in even a small way. For us, what that looked like in the short term: openly talking about the murder of George Floyd and systemic racism, contributing to organizations that help the Black community, sharing resources (many of them from Dr. Laura Quiros!), having a company day off for rest and research, and scheduling facilitated forums and dialogues with Laura.

Knowing all my White friends were asking themselves what to do, simply telling White employees what to do seemed helpful. If we can provide them with a direction to aim their energies, we are helping in even a small way. And as a result, hopefully helping tear down systemic racism that shows up in the world and within the organization (which, of course, contributes to how it shows up in the world).

It also gives me a better understanding of how some White employees (and we are majority White) may interact with non-white employees and how that could create a less inclusive working environment for people. For example: a complete lack of understanding of what someone else may be going through. In a discussion with White friends, one friend brought up an example of a Black classmate in high school who was accepted to a college program that he was not accepted to. His first reaction was that that person was likely accepted because he was Black. As time has passed not getting into that program has not affected my friend at all in his ability to succeed. During this conversation he spoke openly about this and how he wished he could speak with his younger self.

I was later able to use this example with a White colleague who brought up "reverse racism" as an example of how "reverse racism" is not real. I believe it helped my White colleague better understand it. These personal conversations with White friends can be brought into the workplace as examples to help other White people better understand.

As an organization we can help people flex the muscle of empathy and I see it having ripple effects across the organization for inclusion and how we work. If we increase empathy, we make Respondent more inclusive, we help everyone work better together.

This work is multifaceted and the more we can bring it into our personal lives the better our organizations will be and vice versa. I think personal work is especially helpful for those in leadership positions because it sets the tone, but can also be incredibly helpful for White employees at all levels of the business. If White employees are better able to understand how their Whiteness shows up outside of work, they can then understand how it shows up inside of work and take steps to own and alter things that add to systemic racism inside and outside of work.

Case Study: Biracial Woman Social Work Supervisor: An Example of Positive Disruption

The next case study is written from the lens of a biracial woman Social Work Supervisor in a non-profit organization. This particular woman was once my doctoral student and since she finished the program, we have stayed in touch on and off throughout the years.

During her time in my class we shared a commonality in our racial identity development which helped move her work to a deeper place of engagement. Her racial identity was not siloed from her studies. We recently facilitated a session together for supervisors focusing on trauma-informed supervision. During one of our preparatory calls for the workshop we were facilitating together she asked me how to handle a situation regarding a conversation on race, she had recently experienced with her supervisor. My initial question to her when she was sharing was, what would you have done differently? My next question was what feeling surfaced for you? My practice with her was from a trauma-informed diversity and inclusion lens. Evoking the tenets of trauma-informed practice, helping her to explicitly name her feelings, connect them to her experience as a mixed-race woman while acknowledging the power dynamic in the relationship, as she was struggling with a senior manager in a position of power. There was a felt precarity from her and an adherence to the traditional hierarchy of social work practice where questioning a supervisor is not normative, all of which originally caused her to stay silent. Yet, as you will read in the case study below, she revisited the incident after she leaned into her supports with another woman of color social work educator to process her feelings. You, the reader, have permission to process feelings and return to the experience at a later time. Students often think that they cannot go back and revisit situations but sometimes we are not brave in that exact moment and it takes a little time to re-group and locate ourselves in order to sincerely engage without the emotional armor or defensiveness. She explains what happened below.

> As a mixed-race woman of color and mid-level manager within my organization, I was recently asked to facilitate a virtual meeting with members of our racial awareness group in the wake of the murder of George Floyd. The meeting consisted of approximately 15 people where 3 or 4 people were white and the others were people of color. During the meeting, one of the White women spoke about her reactions to the murder, however, most others who spoke were Black or Brown. When asked by a Black participant if she would like to say something, one of the other White participants, a senior manager, verbalized that she would be staying silent during the meeting because she felt she should not speak due to her

White privilege. When the meeting ended the White woman who did speak at the meeting reached out to me asking if she had done something wrong. After validating her experience, I suggested that there is no clear right or wrong way to respond and we started a dialogue about the role of White voices within these discussions.

The next day I felt uncomfortable and slightly angry. After processing these feelings with a valued mentor, educator, researcher and DEI consultant I felt compelled to provide feedback to the senior manager and requested a meeting to do so. Fortunately, the senior manager was receptive, and I expressed my thoughts and feelings about how her statement landed with me and with the White employee (who had given me permission to share her experience). After acknowledging the senior manager's commitment to create safe and brave spaces for courageous conversations within our organization, I shared my belief that staying silent is a privilege and suggested that other White people would likely follow her lead and also stay silent. We were able to share our thoughts and ideas about this in a mutually respectful way. Ultimately, she thanked me for having the courage to challenge her and we each vowed to continue to work together in our efforts to decrease racism within our agency.

Case Study: Black Woman Head of Human Resources: The Power of Relationship Building

This final Case Study speaks to the power of relationship building while in the role of a coach for a non-profit organization. Although this reads more as a testimonial than a case study, I choose it to illustrate that this works involves a use of self and a level of intimacy that cuts across traditional social work boundaries. It was written to me and for me, by the Head of Human Resources, A Black woman whom I befriended during my work. She was the person who brought me on to work with executive leadership and help co-facilitate the organizations' diversity, equity and inclusion council. Due to the nature of the work of this non-profit, there was a need for a consultant who had expertise in both trauma and diversity and inclusion. I find in my role as a consultant I have developed strong relationships with Black and Brown women who occupy Executive Leadership roles and are often the only person of color in that leadership space. It is a fast bond and one that helps me navigate the white organizational spaces as I use my privilege as a consultant to positively disrupt, name the places white supremacy lives and the inherent traumas associated with being the only Black person in a leadership role. As she explains:

> In this climate of unrest being the only woman of color on the senior leadership team poses a number of challenges that those who are not in my position could relate. Questioning how to navigate in this space without losing my mind, my sense of self and questioning whether I belong here.
>
> My saving grace is being able to not only have a personal but just as important a professional support system from one who can relate. Navigating in a space that has often times created days of despair, the frustrations of, yet again teaching white folks the impact of systemic racism, the continued frustrations of teaching common decency. Only those that are able to look through that same lens can truly understand the inward pain that for so long could not publicly be expressed.
>
> The likelihood of developing a friendship at this later stage in my life, I could not remotely perceive. Laura appeared at just the right time and in retrospect moving forward in this work and the world we live in, I could not phantom not having her support and validation. I have confirmation that I am not losing my mind. I am not alone. We are not alone. And, our voices will be heard as we continue to grow and support each other.

CONCLUSION
The Work Begins at Home

Community Engagement

In the summer of 2019, I joined the Diversity, Equity and Inclusion committee at my local YMCA. The same YMCA that my daughters have attended their whole lives for camp and before and after school programming. The Montclair, New Jersey YMCA has been a safe haven for my family during the most difficult times and that was my reasoning for wanting to join this committee. As you have read in this book, my life's work is grounded in trauma-informed practice, with an explicit lens on and integration of social justice, diversity and inclusion and I wanted to share myself and this work with and in my community. My motivation to join this committee also stemmed from the fact that social workers are community organizers. During the spring of 2020 I was asked to chair the committee along with two other members who would serve as co-chairs, a white cisgender woman named Kimberly Marsh and a cisgender Black man named Mike Chiles. Kimberly works in the corporate diversity and inclusion space. She is humble and validating of the experiences Mike and I share as people of color and members of the community. She is a mother to a young boy close in age to my youngest daughter Isabel. Kimberly is always working on deepening her knowledge of her whiteness, her unearned privilege and ways to sincerely show up an ally. Mike Chiles is an educator and a staple in the Montclair community having served as a leader in the public-school system for years and truly a pillar of our community. Our committee meetings often turn into a support group as we always end up sharing stories of how the COVID-19 pandemic and racial trauma has impacted us personally and professionally. It is an honor to serve beside both of them and in collaboration take a deep dive into how our Montclair, New Jersey community is also complicit in upholding the status quo, despite its reputation of diversity and inclusion. It is a very different experience for me to do this work in my own community. Similar to conversations I have had to have with my mom about our racial and cultural differences, there is an intimacy and vulnerability involved in my community organizing work that feels unique and separate from the work I do in organizations where I serve just as a consultant. In this space, I represent my family and my friends while actively working to bring an anti-racist lens to help improve the quality of peoples' lives where I live.

Shortly after the resurgence of the Black Lives Matter movement, I helped our YMCA CEO craft a message to send to the community. The message touched on the responsibility of the YMCA to be a place of inclusion and uphold a mission of social justice. The message spoke to the leaders in the community, the parents, the Black, Indigenous, people of color and the white members. We also held forums for the community that I facilitated along with the support from my co-chairs and other members of the committee and the Board of Directors focused on process and action toward racial equity. The work in my community brings me gratitude, a sense of belonging and a responsibility unlike any other. I believe that as long as I live in this community, my work with the YMCA is an investment in my children's' future along with other generations. To help contribute a voice and perspective that is often on the margins where you live, is priceless. The work begins at home.

My Heart Space

I have stated in the book that in order to sincerely engage in social justice work, it has to come from your heart. I have two daughters and they have different dads. My oldest daughters' father is white and my youngest daughters' father is Black and Trinidadian. They both have strong relationships with their dads in very different ways, all of which is very culture specific. We have spent a lot of time in our home nurturing the Black girl joy in my little one. She is a free spirit; seen in the way she wears her hair, to how she always seems to be moving to the music in her head. In the summer time she often rides her bike barefoot, loves drawing rainbows, unicorns and mermaids and creates stories in her head to play out with her dolls all of whom have names and sometimes join us at the dinner table and long car rides. My oldest daughter is twelve and I have had the opportunity during this time of quarantine to watch her navigate classrooms discussions and friendships. She is maternal by nature, a skilled athlete, a loyal friend and has been with me through some very difficult moments. We communicate a lot and openly, and she has no problem challenging me during times I may have come down too hard on her. She also has had the opportunity to watch me work these last 2 months. She's able and welcome to listen in on conversations with my colleagues, students and leaders I work with. It never occurred to me just how much she was taking it in until recently. As parents, we are sometimes afforded those unique opportunities to see the learnings of our parenting. I overheard her on a call with her class and I heard her share her reactions to the murder of George Floyd, while also questioning her classmates and teachers as to why people suddenly care now when racism has always been here. Her reasoning fell along the lines of maybe people just have more time now because they are home. I then heard her make a statement in response to a comment one of the other students made; she said "even people who do not support Trump are not aware of their white privilege. Maybe it has nothing to do with if she supported Trump or not, maybe she just does not see her white privilege." We spoke about this after, as we often recap the day. It was a natural response for her. Meaning, she not only understands the language of white privilege, but is also able to put it into her own words and recognize it in her 12-year-old world. She also understands and welcomes her responsibility to name racism and normalize discussions of white privilege, in part because her sister is Black.

The question I pose to you all at this moment is, do we also have the courage to begin these conversations of racial trauma and social justice in our home. Do we care enough about Black people and their experiences to make ourselves uncomfortable and relinquish some of our privilege? Do we have the courage to speak about the subtle ways that white unearned advantage shows up in everyday experiences and conversations? Do we have the courage to positively disrupt white and normative spaces that are inherently exclusive? This is the work, every day. Are we walking in protests and marches and then taking that fervor and momentum home with us to sit quietly and take an intentional and internal look at how we have been complicit in upholding white supremacy?

In this project, I am asking you to disrupt the unnamed ideologies and spaces that dictate so much of our lives. I shared my narrative with you along the way as a way to see how our ancestral history and experiences that begin in the home, impact how we show up as social work students, at our internships, at work and how we lead. For social workers specifically, I encourage you to revisit your purpose for why you decided to purpose social work as a career, and keep challenging that and reflecting on that. For white social workers in particular, this is the moment for you to continue to, or begin to, use yourself to disrupt white normative spaces in your classrooms, personal spheres and in your work. I am writing to you now in this moment and movement of change when we are staring directly at racial trauma experience by BIPOC. I took my daughters to a local protest in our community, and I was explaining to them that I spent much of my last year of my Masters of Social Work program marching against police brutality. It was February of 1999, 21 years ago, when 4 plain clothes officers shot 41 bullets at a 23-year-old man named Amado Diallo outside of his apartment building in Bronx, New York. While I recognize that many social workers worked on the front line during the COVID-19 pandemic, I also want to recognize those who spent time protesting, marching and taking a deep internal look at how we have all been complicit in upholding systemic racism.

We are dealing with complex trauma. Meaning, the timing of the event combined with the multiple exposures, in this case a health crisis and racial trauma, can destabilize core elements of the self. My colleague Dr. Roni Berger writes about the concept of posttraumatic growth in her book; *Stress, Trauma and Posttraumatic Growth: Social Context, Environment and Identities* (Berger, 2015). Her area of research touches on the growth that comes from trauma. Instead of thinking of trauma as a deficit, we see it as an opportunity to expand in ways we did not even know were possible. Using myself as a model to how this theory and practice comes alive, I think of all of my traumatic experiences I have shared with you in the project. The passing of my brother, the exclusion I experienced and felt from my parents, the impact of divorce and abuse as a young child, the experiences of discrimination in the workplace, and the trauma I experienced as a result of my two divorces. All of these experiences in their own ways have led me to a career where my lens and my practice is that of positive disruption, inclusion and healing. Where I remain hypervigilant to creating spaces in my classrooms and the organizations I work with, that are brave, compassionate, vulnerable, trauma responsive, where there is an understanding of nuance, where we can honor curiosity and be responsive to the trauma in the space. My relationship with my mother who was not aware of or skilled at owning the many unearned advantages she gains from being white has allowed me to enter this work from a place of compassion. I can relate to and understand white social workers and executives in particular, from a more compassionate and personal level, while also holding them accountable. Understanding and gaining comfort with nuance is, in a certain respect, forced upon you when you grow up and live on and outside the margins of socially constructed identities. I have compassion for this and at the same time, have a felt responsibility to help my mother, the students and the clients I work with, see that privilege and the ways those unearned advantages have caused harm and trauma for Black, Indigenous and people of color. Being Black, Indigenous or a person of color in predominantly white spaces is traumatic in and of itself. How do we as social workers and leaders create the cultures to hold that, nurture that, and actively fight against the status quo and white supremacy systems that support that trauma? Can we lean into that Revolutionary Love we named earlier?

I continue to wonder how will this moment be remembered by white historians? What is possible? It is so easy for things not to change because the roots of white supremacy run deep. Conversations with my Black and Brown friends reveal that living in this moment of the COVID-19 pandemic and watching and experiencing the complex trauma all at once is triggering and incredibly emotionally, psychologically and spiritually draining. Yet, I have to embrace this moment as an opportunity for positive disruption on every level. As social workers we are grounded in a mission of social justice and that does not, and cannot continue to, allow for the upholding of the status quo. Our use of self as transformational leaders is paramount in living up to this mission. Coming full circle from where we started, this is my purpose, to deliver this text to you in an effort to help disrupt spaces of exclusion and create spaces of inclusion and healing. True to my culture, I really do believe we are all here for a reason, and this is my reason.

REFERENCES

Abrams, L. S., & Moio, J. A. (2009). Critical race theory and the cultural competence dilemma in social work education. *Journal of Social Work Education*, 45(2), 245–261.

Ahmed, S. (2012). *On being included: Racism and diversity in institutional life*. London, UK: Duke University Press.

Anzaldua, G. (1987). *Borderlands/La frontera: The new mestiza*. Iowa City, IA: Aunt Lute Books.

Berger, R. (2015). *Stress, trauma, and posttraumatic growth: Social context, environment, and identities*. New York, NY: Routledge.

Bonilla-Silva, E. (2010). *Racism without racists: Color-blind racism and racial inequality in contemporary America*. Lanham, MD: Rowman & Littlefield.

Brach, T. P. (2003). *Radical acceptance: Embracing your life with the heart of a Buddha*. New York, NY: Bantam.

Brown, B. (2018). *Dare to lead*. New York, NY: Random House.

Bryant, H. (2018). *The heritage: Black athletes, a divided America, and the politics of patriotism*. Boston, MA: Beacon Press.

Burstow, B. (2003). Toward a radical understanding of trauma and trauma work. *Violence against Women*, 9(11), 1293–1317.

Butler, J. (2015). *Notes toward a performative theory of assembly*. London, UK: Harvard University Press.

Carli, L. L., & Eagly, A. H. (2016). Women face a labyrinth: An examination of metaphors for women leaders. *Gender in Management: An International Journal*, *31*(8), 514–527.

Carter, M. Z., Mossholder, K. W., Feild, H. S., & Armenakis, A. A. (2014). Transformational leadership, interactional justice, and organizational citizenship behavior: The effects of racial and gender dissimilarity between supervisors and subordinates. *Group & Organizational Management*, *39*(6), 691–719.

Chin, J. L., & Sanchez-Hucles, J. (2007). Diversity and leadership. *American Psychologist*, *62*(6), 608–609.

Crenshaw, K. (1989). Demarginalizing the intersection of race and sex: A Black feminist critique of antidiscrimination doctrine, feminist theory and antiracist politics. *University of Chicago Legal Forum*.

Darder, A. (2002). *Reinventing Paulo Freire: A pedagogy of love*. Cambridge, UK: The Perseus Books.

Denzin, N. K., & Lincoln, Y. S. (Eds.). (1994). *Handbook of qualitative research*. Thousand Oaks CA: Sage Publications.

DiAngelo, R. (2018). *White fragility*. Boston, MA: Beacon Press.

DuBois, W. E. B. (1903/1963/2003). *The souls of Black folk*. New York, NY: Fine Creative.

Fallot, R. D. (2011). *Creating cultures of trauma-informed care. Substance abuse and mental health services administration (SAMHSA)*. Treatment for Homeless Program Workshop.

Festekjian, A., Tram, S., Murray, C. B., Sy, T., & Huynh, H. P. (2014). I see me the way you see me: The influence of race on interpersonal and intrapersonal leadership perceptions. *Journal of Leadership & Organizational Studies*, *21*(1), 102–119.

Gassam, J. (2019, December 29). Your unconscious bias trainings keep failing because you're not addressing systemic bias. *Forbes*. https://www.forbes.com/sites/janicegassam/2020/12/29/your-unconscious-bias-trainings-keep-failing-because-youre-not-addressing-systemic-bias/#c862c9c1e9d3

Gokhale, K., & Geeta, J. (2015). Leadership: An important domain in social work education. *Social Work Footprints*.

Gundemir, S., Homan, A. C., de Dreu, C. K., & van Vugt, M. (2014). Think leader, think White? Capturing and weakening an implicit pro-White leadership bias. *PLoS One*, 9(1), e83915.

Herman, J. (1997). *Trauma and recovery.* New York, NY: Basic Books.

Hite, L. M. (2007). Hispanic women managers and professionals: Reflections on life and work. *Gender, Work and Organization*, 14(1), 20–36.

hooks, b (1994). *Teaching to transgress.* New York, NY: Routledge.

hooks, b (2010). *Teaching critical thinking.* New York, NY: Routledge.

Hunang-Nissen, S. (1999). *Dialogue groups: A practical guide to facilitate diversity conversation.* Blue Hill, NE: Medicine Bear Publishing.

Jackson, J. (2005). *Real Black: Adventures in racial sincerity.* Chicago: University of Chicago Press.

Kapuku, R. (2019, September 3). Why performative diversity agendas are failing the most marginalised communities. *Medium*, p. 1. https://medium.com/@reneekapuku/why-performative-diversity-agendas-are-failing-the-most-marginalised-communities-aaff56024b14

Kendi, I. X. (2019). *How to be an anti-racist.* New York, NY: Penguin Random House.

King, R. C., & DaCosta, K. (1996). Changing face, changing race: The remaking of race in Japanese American and African American communities. In M. P. P. Root (Ed.), *The multiracial experience: Racial borders as the new frontier* (pp. 227–244). Newbury Park, CA: Sage Publications.

Lindsey, M. (2019, July 6). *Dallas News.* Available at https://www.dallasnews.com/news/education/2019/07/06/how-this-texas-college-gives-every-single-student-help-with-trauma-mental-health/

Liu, H., & Baker, C. (2016). White knights: Leadership as the heroicisation of whiteness. *Leadership*, 12(4), 420–448.

Lorde, A. (1983). There is no hierarchy of oppression. *Bulletin: Homophobia and Education*, 14, 9.

Love, B. (2013). Developing a liberatory consciousness. In W. B. M. Adams (Ed.), *Readings for diversity and social justice* (pp. 601–605). New York, NY: Routledge.

Lowe, F. (2013). Keeping leadership White: Invisible blocks to Black leadership and its denial in White organizations. *Journal of Social Work Practice*, 27(2), 149–162.

Mbembe, A. (2019). *Necropolitics.* Durham, NC: Duke University Press.

McIntosh, P. (1988). White privilege: Unpacking the invisible White knapsack. *White Privilege and Male Privilege: A Personal Account of Coming to See Correspondences Through Work in Women's.* Available at: https://www.racialequitytools.org/resourcefiles/mcintosh.pdf

McLaren, P. (2000). *Che guevara, Paulo Freire and the pedagogy of the revolution.* Lanham, MD: Rowman and Littlefield.

Menaken, R. (2017). *My Grandmother's Hands: Racialized trauma and the pathway to mending our hearts and bodies.* Las Vegas, NV: Central Recovery Press.

Najavits, L. (2002). *Seeking safety: A treatment manual for PTSD and substance abuse.* New York, NY: Guildford Press.

NASW. (n.d.). *Code of Ethics.* Retrieved from https://www.socialworkers.org/about/ethics/code-of-ethics/code-of-ethics-english.

Okun, T. (n.d.). *Dismantling Racism.* Retrieved from http://www.dismantlingracism.org/white-supremacy-culture.html

Okun, T., & Jones, K. (2001). *White Supremacy Organizational Culture.* Retrieved from Dismantling Racism. Available at: https://www.showingupforracialjustice.org/white-supremacy-culture-characteristics.html

Patton, L. D., & Haynes, C. M. (2014). Using critical interpretive lenses to examine glass ceiling effects through qualitative research. *New Directions for Institutional Research, 2013*(159), 25–35.

Quiros, L. (2012). Raising the voice: Teaching through a multicultural Lens. *Journal of Teaching in Social Work, 32*(5), 518–531.

Quiros, L., & Araujo Dawson, B. (2013). The color paradigm: The impact of colorism on the racial identity and identification of Latinas. *Journal of Human Behavior in the Social Environment, 23*(3), 10.

Quiros, L., & Berger, R. (2013). Responding to the sociopolitical complexity of trauma: An integration of theory and practice. *Journal of Loss and Trauma: International Perspectives on Stress & Coping,* 20(2), 149–159.

Quiros, L., Varghese, R., & Vanidestine, T. (2020). Disrupting the single story: Challenging dominant trauma narratives through a critical race lens. *Traumatology, 26*(2), 160–168.

Sanchez-Hucles, J. V., & Davis, D. D. (2010). Women and women of color in leadership: Complexity, identity, and intersectionality. *American Psychologist,* 65(3), 171–181.

Savage, A., Quiros, L., Dodd, S. J. & Bonavota, D. (2007). Building trauma informed practice: Appreciating the impact of trauma in the lives of women with substance abuse and mental health problems. *Journal of Social Work Practice in the Addictions,* 7(1-2), 91–116.

Schiele, J. H. (2007). Implications of the equality-of-oppressions paradigm for curriculum content on BIPOC. *Journal of Social Work Education, 43*(1), 83–100.

Varghese, R. (2016). Teaching to transform: Addressing race and racism in the teaching of clinical social work practice. *Journal for Social Work Education*, 52, S134–S147.

Warner, J., Ellmann, N., & Boesch, D. (2018). *The Women's Leadership Gap*. Center for American Progress.

Welang, N. (2018). Triple consciousness: The reimagination of Black female identities in contemporary American culture. *Open Cultural Studies*, *2*(1), 296–306.

Wheeler, A. (2020, February 5). 'Fake Diversity': Barnes & Noble cancels race-swapped covers. *The Guardian*. Available at https://www.theguardian.com/books/2020/feb/05/barnes-and-noble-diverse-classics-backlash

Yee, J. Y. (2005). Critical anti-racism praxis: The concept of Whiteness implicated. In S. Hicks, J. Fook, & R. Pozzuto (Eds.), *Social work: A critical turn* (pp. 87–103). Toronto, Ontario, Canada: Thompson Educational Publishing.

Zelevansky, N. (2019, November 20). The big business of unconscious bias. *The New York Times*. Available at: https://www.nytimes.com/2019/11/20/style/diversity-consultants.html

INDEX